Not by the Seat of My Pants!

Not by the Seat of My Pants!

Leadership Lessons for the Call Center Supervisor

Anne G. Nickerson

iUniverse, Inc.
New York Lincoln Shanghai

Not by the Seat of My Pants!
Leadership Lessons for the Call Center Supervisor

iUniverse, Inc.

For information address:
iUniverse, Inc.
2021 Pine Lake Road, Suite 100
Lincoln, NE 68512
www.iuniverse.com

ISBN: 0-595-32366-9

Printed in the United States of America

Contents

Preface

Writing a book has been my dream and goal for more than 20 years. This book was born as I coached clients, answered questions at conferences, and observed how most supervisors learn to do their job—by the seat of their pants!

The unsung hero of the workplace is the front line supervisor. Customers must be satisfied so they will continue to purchase products and services. Productivity must be balanced with quality. Workflow and systems must be woven together for a smooth operation. People need to be developed to perform at their best, and individuals require motivation to consistently work together. Blending these critical job elements is not an easy task, and learning how to manage them should not be left to chance. The path to becoming an inspired leader is forged with the support of good coaching, training and awareness of opportunities around you.

This book is a fictional story used to illustrate leadership principles. It is meant to be fun to read, as well as a realistic and practical guide for the call center supervisor. Chris, the main character and story narrator, is an agent-turned-boss, who encounters a wide array of situations and challenges commonly faced by most supervisors. Stephanie, the insightful coach, consistently demonstrates how effective coaching can influence and develop a supervisor. The other characters who comprise the work-team have personalities, issues and conversations that will make the reader reflect upon their own work experiences with affection. Though all characters are fictional, they have traits and personalities recognizable to all readers!

While the characters are fictional, they are created from my years of living, breathing and leading customer service and sales. The book provides a smorgasbord of ideas that have worked for me and many clients with thousands of employees in the trenches who have adopted the lessons. Designed for flexibility and different learning styles, the book is organized into chapters with sub-headings for readers who need to find nuggets of information quickly. Or, the story can be read from cover-to-cover to give hope to the new or veteran supervisor who needs proof that, at the end of the day, the job can be successfully accomplished.

You may find a "silver bullet" for just the situation you're dealing with, or a seed of an idea to plant and germinate. Either way, my wish is that this book offers supervisors hope, guidance, a brighter future, and a truly enriched experience as they journey through their own transitions and lessons.

Acknowledgements

Not by the Seat of My Pants! Leadership Lessons for the Call Center Supervisor is the culmination of years of coaching, training and living the challenges we face as supervisors in today's workplace. It has been a passion-driven goal during which I've had the privilege and honor of working with the most incredible, talented, devoted and caring supervisors who have worked tirelessly to bring the best they have to the people they serve.

This book would not have been possible without the efforts and support of many awesome individuals. I am grateful for their patience, commitment, brilliant feedback, ideas, loving support and encouragement when I needed it the most.

Eternal hugs to my daughter, Stephanie, for your patience and understanding when mom needed "five more minutes" to finish another paragraph, or one more call to speak with a client who was in need of coaching. You continue to teach me lessons in balance and tenacity. I know you will be an exceptional leader when your time comes.

I'm forever grateful to Peter, my husband, partner, confidant and friend who is constantly in my corner. Your sense of humor, pride in my work, giving me the freedom to take healthy risks, and forever sustaining me when I was in doubt about my ideas was often what I needed to persevere. You are an incredible business advisor and leader in your own right.

A special thanks to my friend and associate, Holly, for taking care of all of the details so I could stay focused on writing. Your tireless work on organization, flow, and editing was invaluable. Your ability to keep track of the ever-changing to-do list and keeping me on deadline, always with an infectious positive attitude, is truly a gift. Your willingness to persevere with the reading and formatting of this work along with your persistence and patience with the computer gremlins helped me keep my sanity.

Heartwarming thanks to my sister, Nancy, who after reading the draft of the first chapter gave me candid feedback to make it 'more real'; your encouragement and ideas have helped create authentic characters throughout the book so the reader can see themselves in similar situations. I can always count on your listening ear, and especially appreciate the examples of dialogue, support on creating the charts, analytics and practical technical explanations.

Thanks to the members of my advisory board for your endless time and support: Sarah Kennedy, Partner, Service Quality Measurement and Co-Founder Customer Contact Strategy Forum, for your keen insights, marketing ideas, cheerful confidence and time helping with the content in Chapter 11; Beth Marchetti, Information Service Center Manager for the American Board of Internal Medicine, for testing ideas with your supervisors, sending me information to include, and especially for your candid feedback; and Kate Powell, Vice President at PNC Bank, for your strategic perspective and sincere advice.

Thanks to Judy Feld, my personal mentor and business coach, for your unwavering commitment to helping me get my messages and work into the world. Thanks for being a passionate supporter and honest source of feedback in all that I strive to do.

I thank Ken and his team from PortONE Internet for thinking through all of the details for my web site, your intuition and research about the market, technical support and advice and always meeting our tight deadlines.

My utmost gratitude to Sid Simon, Merrill Harmin, and Dan Dana for the long-term teaching you've each provided me, as well as your unwavering support to include much of what I learned from you in this book.

My heartfelt thanks to Kathy DeCastro, my esteemed friend and colleague, for your human resource counsel, creativity, friendship and encouragement at just the right moments.

Grazie to Tim McClernon, my respected friend and colleague, for your willingness to hear out my endless ideas, helping me stay focused on my most critical work, along with your eye for design and marketing advice.

Special thanks to literary editors extraordinaire, Rhonda Proctor and Jennifer Loper from The Proctor Consortium, for your advocacy, tireless reviews, and for sharing in the vision of creating a book for meeting the learning needs of supervisors. And thanks to my illustrator, Mardis Bagley, for capturing the essence of the purpose of this book in the cover design and graphics.

Thanks to my proofreaders Ron Blanchette, Nancy Tirabassi, Pat Scheg, and Sally Crosiar for your eagle eyes and thoughtful suggestions.

My utmost appreciation to my parents, Mary and Francis, for your unending love and support. Your encouragement, belief in me, and your model of work ethic, leadership, honesty, business savvy, and people management have all served as a foundation for my own success.

To Janet at iUniverse for her patience and promptness, answering all our questions and helping me to learn the ropes from the publishing side of creating a book.

To all of the many colleagues I've worked with over the years—this book is a culmination of all that you've taught me. Thank you for sharing your gifts.

Finally, let me acknowledge and thank you—the reader, who intuitively knew that something important was waiting for you when you chose to pick up this book. I hope that even one small idea or lesson you obtain from reading this story helps you in your own journey and transition to become an inspirational and successful supervisor and leader.

1

The Job Is Mine!

I entered my new workspace on my first day as Team Leader. Colleagues had decorated the area with balloons, streamers and welcome signs, along with a signed card from everyone wishing me luck in my new position. It was official. I was now a part of the management team in the recently reorganized Sales and Service Contact Center for Power Solutions, Inc.

My hands trembled with excitement as I thought about all the opportunities in front of me. I now had the chance to make a *difference* in this fast-growing company.

All my friends had encouraged me to apply when the job posting went up on the break room wall. I hesitated at first, since I had no previous management experience—at least no formal training that I thought necessary for such a critical job. My friend Lily had also applied for the job, and it was a difficult decision to apply, knowing I would be in direct competition with her. But the company was looking for someone who knew our products and customers, and who had a successful track record servicing and selling to difficult people. I understood all of these areas well, since my sales had been in the top 10% during the past two years and I had served on the escalation team, taking the toughest, angriest and most dissatisfied customer calls. I had learned a lot over the last few years, and hoped to change some of the processes and systems that made an associate's job more difficult. I was also eager to share my passion to create some new products that our customers desperately wanted!

After three weeks of paperwork and interviews, I had won the job! I knew that I was hired because of my rapport with customers and my successful selling skills. Now my job would be to help other agents achieve the same wonderful results.

On my first morning as a Supervisor, I was a bit nervous. I came to work early to set up my new office and determine what I needed to do first. I was thinking about how I was going to work on my relationship with Lily and, at some point, help her advance into a supervisory role, as well as how I was going to interact with my friends who were now a part of my team, when I saw my phone flashing.

I answered, "Hello, this is Chris Crandall. How may I help you?"

"Chris, this is David." David was a supervisor, and now one of my counterparts, who I had known for years. He had been with the company for quite a while and was well respected by all levels of the organization. "I saw you drive into the parking garage, and wanted to be the first to welcome you to our supervisory team," he said. "We're really counting on you to help us meet the new revenue objectives and coach this team on selling and satisfying customers' needs—just like *you* did, star!"

"Well, thanks David," I replied. "I'm really excited to be here and looking forward to doing just that! I was just setting up my office and reading my e-mails when you called. I see a note here that I have an appointment at 9 a.m. with my new coach, Stephanie Haley. She's going to help me learn the ropes and act as a resource for my questions. As I recall, she was your coach when you became a supervisor. What was your experience like with her?"

Enthusiastically, David said, "You'll really like Stephanie. She has a reputation as one of the best coaches for a new supervisor. She'll help you get the most from your team, enjoy your work, and keep life balanced as things continue to 'rock and roll' around here."

"That's good to know," I replied.

"Yeah, Stephanie mentored me when I started leading a team," he went on. "I was taking some classes in business school when I first started the job and, in all of my studies, I learned that success was a combination of skill, talent, and sometimes lots of fancy footwork. And as you know, our company has been growing so quickly that there hasn't been any time for a formal supervisory training program. So having a coach is a lifesaver to navigate through all of the changes that happen when you take the job."

"But what was *your* experience with her?" I asked again.

He chuckled reassuringly. "Chris, you'll get along fine with her," he said. "I can tell you that she asks thoughtful questions that provoke thinking. She has a track record for helping new supervisors exceed their expectations, so you're not operating by the seat of your pants. In fact, she'll keep you *out* of the hot seat!"

My mind strayed for a second. I did have a fear of moving from a *comfortable position* of knowing and familiarity, to the *uncertainty* of operating by the seat of my pants. I also knew that our work culture was very entrepreneurial and that often, when sitting in the associate's chair, I didn't always understand how decisions were made, nor did I always see how they helped the customer. I sure had a lot to learn about the politics of the organization and especially how *not* to alienate my former co-workers during my learning curve.

David interrupted my thoughts. "So, feel free to call me anytime if you have a question about some of the processes or systems here and," he playfully added, "if you just want to bounce ideas around for how we're going to meet our aggressive sales and service goals. Anyway, I'm really glad you're here."

It was clear that David would be a big help to me and a solid support in my transition. I made a mental note to keep in contact and use him as a resource to help me deal with issues and the varied personalities on my new team.

As soon as I hung up, I felt butterflies in my stomach. I was about to join the ranks of my former supervisors, as a *colleague*, not an agent, and needed to help my new team to improve results quickly. How was I going to do this? I knew all kinds of tools and tricks that worked as I sold and serviced customers, but I had never taught anyone else how to use them. Besides, I wasn't sure my techniques would work for anyone else. I just seemed to have a sixth sense when it came to understanding customers, and almost knew before they did what they needed or wanted.

I slowly took a deep breath and said to myself, "This is not the first time you started out blindly, so let's do what you do best, *meet the needs of customers.* Your customers are just different now. Now, your customers are members of your team and the company's management team. You have three groups to please now—direct reports, supervisors and other support departments in the company."

With my personal motivation speech over, I knew that just because I was a supervisor now, others were not going to jump at what I said. I had to slowly gain respect to make progress. I looked at my watch and realized the first step was to get to my meeting on time with Coach Stephanie.

2

Setting Goals with Coach Stephanie

Stephanie was sitting at her desk. She was on the phone, but motioned me in to sit down. I glanced around the room as I took a seat and was immediately intrigued by some of the quotes hanging on her walls:

"Do what you value and value what you do."

"In the confrontation between the stream and the rock, the stream always wins—not through strength, but by perseverance."

She had photos of her kids on her desk and appeared very organized and confident. I immediately sensed that I was going to learn a lot from her. I wondered how she balanced her work and still had time for her family. At some point, I'd have to ask her about the stories behind the quotes.

As she hung up from her phone call, Stephanie cheerfully greeted me, "Hello, Chris. Welcome to your first day on the job!"

Surprisingly, I wasn't feeling apprehensive at all. Stephanie seemed to have the gift of putting people at ease. "Thanks, Stephanie," I said with enthusiasm. "I'm really glad that I'm meeting with you on my *first* day on the job as a supervisor. My head is swimming with questions, and I'm really anxious to get started on the right foot."

Her response relaxed me immediately. "Chris, I'm so glad you were selected for this position. Though we haven't had the opportunity to work together directly, I am familiar with your talents and gifts. We need creative and critical thinkers like you to take our company to the next level." She continued, "I'm glad you have questions. We all do when we start a new role, especially one that is so crucial to the organization. I'm here to help you in any way that I can. So, why don't we start with your questions, and then I'm sure I'll have a few thoughts to share with you along the way."

"OK," I said. This made sense and the butterflies fluttered away. "I've been writing down my ideas all weekend, and they're all over the place. I'm not sure where to start."

Defining the Role of the Coach

Stephanie nodded her head. "How about asking your questions and I'll write them on the board," she said. "We'll see if we can identify categories to help target what we should work on. Then we'll decide which ones to tackle first. How does that sound?"

"Sounds like a plan to me," I said, as I remembered David telling me how Stephanie would help me—she was already helping me organize my thoughts.

"I want you to know that our conversations are confidential," Stephanie explained. "This is important to both of us so that we can be candid for the purpose of solving issues and making good decisions. Would you agree?"

I had wondered how open she would allow me to be with her. "Agreed," I said gladly. I liked the idea of talking to her without worrying about my words coming back to haunt me. I knew she deserved the same protection. I also realized that I needed to be professional, as Stephanie would be giving input into my performance evaluation and that other management team members would ask how I was progressing.

Stephanie walked over to the board, "OK. What's your first question?"

"Well, first I wonder where to draw the line between my friends that I used to work with, who I must now supervise and motivate. I mean, our families get together on weekends, some of us play in the same annual golf tournament and we carpool occasionally. I just know when they hear rumors, they're going to ask me for the inside information and, on some occasions, I realize that information can't be shared."

Stephanie continued to listen and take notes on the board as I rambled. "I'm afraid I may have to start over and create a new group of friends—but I don't really want to drift away from this group," I said. "I don't want to forget the good times, but I think my relationship with them will change. And I'm sure there will come a time when their performance may not meet expectations—and I'll need to coach or maybe even discipline them. You can probably tell I'm really struggling here because I've been buddies with some for a long time, and I'm just not sure what to do.

"And," I continued, "I also know that I need to learn how to coach them, *and* the other team members I don't know yet. When I worked with them as fellow associates, I didn't say much about how they could be doing things better to help our customers. Now, as a supervisor, I'll want to motivate them and get them as excited as I am. But I don't want to come off as arrogant because I'm in this new role. I guess I'm just not really clear about how to be the best coach *and* supervisor, while still keeping old friendships."

Stephanie rapidly made her notes on the board. She nodded. "OK, I've captured everything so far," she said. "What else?"

The next thing on my mind was my relationship with David and the other supervisors. "Now I'll be peers with two people I used to work for—one with management tactics I'm not sure I'm comfortable with, and the other with team-building techniques that I really admire. I want to be a team player, but how do I share what I really think and still be politically correct? I know at least two of the other supervisors were rallying for someone else to be chosen for this position."

Stephanie seemed to be keeping up with me, recording a clear summary of my ramblings on the board, so I continued. "I saw an e-mail this morning from Human Resources stating that they will be sending me applications to review for interviews next week for the open position on my team," I continued. "I have never interviewed anyone before. And I'm wondering, what do you ask? Is there a standard set of questions or something? I've heard there are some questions you *can't* ask, but I really don't know what the rules are. I wonder how I'll know if a person is the best job fit, or if they're just good at selling themselves."

I recalled my earlier pep-talk from David, "And, of course, we've got aggressive revenue goals and service goals to meet," I said. "I'm pretty good at keeping my priorities straight, and I've managed small projects in the past, but everything seems urgent right now and big at the same time. I want to do a good job and not let anyone down."

I took a breath and continued, "I'm concerned about my family, too. I know that some supervisors are single with no kids and work eighty hours a week. I have a teenager at home. My family wants me to advance and grow in my job, but they also want me home sometimes. They're concerned that they'll never see me anymore. It all just seems a little bit overwhelming, and I don't like operating by the seat of my pants." I concluded. "I want to do a superb job so that I help the company get results, *and* can grow with it into the future."

I must have looked exhausted, because that's when Stephanie smiled and sat back down.

Setting Goals

She looked at me with a twinkle in her eye. "Chris, I'm impressed with the amount of thinking you've done," she said. "You've actually just completed the first step in identifying the issues that need to be solved. I'm here as your supporter and cheerleader and to help identify solutions, actions and resources for each issue. Let me assure you that your concerns are normal for anyone in their first supervisory role. I'm here to help you come up with a game plan. You also have your boss, Peter, and the others on your team who will lend you insight."

I breathed a sigh of relief.

"Let's take a look at the board," Stephanie said. "As you were sharing your questions, I jotted them down in these key areas," she said, pointing to the list on the board:

- *You're the New Boss*

- *Coaching Customer Interactions*

- *Team Work—All Hands on Deck*

- *Solving Problems and Conflicts*

- *Balancing Work and Family Life*

- *Managing My Future*

"And I'm adding a few that you didn't mention because, based upon my experience with other new supervisors, I know you'll need to consider these too," she said. She gestured to the board again:

- *Human Resources*

- *Time Management*

Stephanie turned around from the board and said, "What do you think, Chris? Does that about capture it?"

"Yes," I said, marveling at her ability to succinctly make a list of what had been whirling around in my head since I received the call from the Human Resources Department weeks before. "If we can figure this all out in one session, I'll be thrilled."

Stephanie said, laughing, "Well, we can perform *some* magic, but I don't think we'll get all of these resolved in one session! In fact, I was just asked to lead another project as well, so while I want to be available to you whenever you need a sounding board, I know that my schedule will be a bit tight for a while. We'll start out by meeting daily, then weekly. We'll work out the schedule conflicts as we go forward. Now, let's figure out where to start."

"That sounds good." I said.

"As your coach," Stephanie continued, "it's important that we work together on what is important to *you*! Take a few minutes to think about the list, and then let's prioritize what you want to focus on first."

We both looked at the list for a minute. I was grateful for a few moments to gather my thoughts and identify my highest priorities. I spent the next few minutes telling Stephanie how I thought the list should be reordered.

When I was finished, I felt as if a weight had been lifted from my shoulders! I finally knew where to begin:

- *How to Coach*
- *You're the New Boss*
- *Team Work—All Hands on Deck*
- *Human Resources*
- *Time and Problem Management*
- *Balancing Work and Family Life*
- *Solving Conflicts*
- *Managing My Future*

"This is a full list, Chris, but all do-able. Not all at once, but," Stephanie stressed, "*over time.*" She reached into her desk and pulled out a journal and handed it to me. "I'd like you to take this journal and jot down these eight issues on the first page."

The hard-covered journal had the words "New Supervisor Gems" written on the cover.

"I like to give this journal to all the new supervisors I'm coaching," she said. "Many have told me that it's been a really helpful tool. By writing down goals and thoughts, it's easy to track what you're doing, note new questions that come up in between our meetings, and look back a year from now and celebrate your progress."

"This is just what I need to get organized," I said. "I always perform better when I have a road map to guide me. Thanks."

As I started writing, I caught myself and said, "You know, I think I should switch the first two around, since the first supervisory meeting is tomorrow morning."

"Good," she said. "So let's take a look at the first item. By the end of the supervisory meeting tomorrow, what would you like to have happened?"

"Well, I know that revenue goals and the new marketing campaign are on the agenda," I said, "and Marketing has just released two new campaigns, so we're being bombarded with calls. I need to understand the revenue targets and why they're so aggressive. At least, I think they are aggressive, but I don't really know how the senior management staff arrived at the numbers. I want to understand the 'why' and the 'what' before I think about solutions."

"True enough. What else?" Stephanie asked.

"Well," I continued, "the training that we just finished on the new computer system was helpful but they were still working the kinks out during training. So I don't think anyone has a complete understanding of how to move smoothly through the new screens and quickly find critical information.

Stephanie nodded, "Um, hmm."

"Just before I was chosen to lead the team, we were getting our ideas together about possible solutions and how to present them to customers. I'd just like to see what the numbers look like, what the high sellers with high customer satisfaction are doing, and what issues the poorer performers are having. Then I'd like us to adjust sales targets over the next *three* months instead of *one* month," I said, feeling relieved.

E + R = O

Stephanie smiled. "These are all excellent ideas, Chris," she said. "What do you think is the best way to present them to the supervisory team?"

"I don't want to come off as the new kid trying to push all my new ideas," I replied, "but I'd like for everyone to recognize the value of the ideas that were generated by the associates before I was promoted. I'm not sure how to do this without potentially alienating someone." I sensed Stephanie would have the right answer.

"Well, you may not always be able to avoid stepping on toes," she said, "but you're on the right path to do some research before you present your idea. Think about how you research a customer's needs before presenting the best solution. You're armed with information, and you know how your solution will benefit the customer. Presenting ideas with the goal to influence a decision is not much different. You're just thinking of ways to best achieve your desired outcome. I have a formula that I'd like you to write in your journal. It's a strategy I originally learned in a workshop with Dr. Sidney B. Simon. Dr. Simon learned the concept from his friend, Jack Canfield who said, in turn, that he had learned it from his former wife, Georgia Nobel."

Stephanie turned to the board, and wrote "E + R = O" and handed me a laminated sheet with a definition. She explained that the "E" represents events; the "R" is how our response is added to the event, to create the "O" or the outcome of the E and R at work together. She noted that the only piece we truly control in this equation is our response, and suggested that, if we think first about the outcome we want, it's much easier to go back and choose how to respond. I made a note in my journal.

Events + Response = Outcome

The only part of the E + R = O equation that we control is our RESPONSE. We don't control the events in our world. If we're clear about the outcome that we want, then our response can create that outcome. So to determine how you want to respond, plan and think about the outcome you'd like to achieve in each situation.

"Here's an example that I know you've experienced with customers," she said. "Let's say that the 'event' is that the customer calls in very upset when they did not receive their delivery on time, and this has had a negative impact on their business. If we respond with apologies and defensiveness, the customer only gets more upset, right?"

I thought about this. Yes, it *was* true. I had many callers tell me that they didn't care about the computer issues we were having, or that shipping from the warehouse was backlogged, and they almost always asked to speak to a supervisor. "You're right, I said to Stephanie. "I've had to learn the hard way that if I empathize with the customer, and let them know they can count on me to fix their problem, they calm down and we quickly work toward a solution. I've resolved a lot of customer issues this way, and earned the right to eventually sell other services."

Brainstorming Rules

"Exactly," Stephanie said with conviction. "So if we apply this same formula to a supervisor or team meeting and think about the outcomes you want to accomplish, you can then back into your plan and decide how you want to respond to concerns and issues that are raised. Let's brainstorm some options on how this can be done. Do you remember the brainstorming guidelines?"

"I think so," I said. "Isn't it to write down all ideas, and keep them all until everyone is finished? Then, you go through the list and pick those that are the best. Oh…and even a wild or impossible idea may spark a solution."

"You're precisely right," she said. "So here's an idea to start. How about meeting with *your* new boss, Peter, before the supervisory meeting, to express your ideas?"

I jumped in. "I could take advantage at the welcome lunch the other supervisors are having for me later today to ask their opinion about what I could do to help meet revenue goals," I said. "Or, I could go to each one and ask about the 'unspoken' meeting rules, and ask for their help in initiating me. On the other hand, I could just wait until the meeting starts, and ask for the meeting ground rules, and suggest my own."

"Yes, or you could do some homework to understand financial returns on our new products and the number of calls we've received since the new marketing campaign started. Then work on watching and learning how the other supervisors reach consensus on goals," Stephanie added.

"I could even create a list of customer needs and product benefits that I heard some of the associates discussing last week, so we could share them across the call center. Like a 'Cheat Sheet'! I could easily show everyone what's been working for me when cross selling the new products," I said enthusiastically.

"All of these are good ideas. Do you have any others?" Stephanie asked.

"Just one more," I said. "I could simply be an observer at the first meeting and just see how things go."

"These are all viable choices," Stephanie said. "Now let's look at them and discuss the benefits and consequences for each one. How about for the last one, being a silent observer?"

Stephanie and I spent the next few minutes discussing the value of each of the options we had brainstormed, and I decided that the best approach for me would be to bring up the subject during the supervisor lunch. Stephanie liked this idea and suggested I make sure to meet with Peter before the supervisory team meeting as well.

"Sure, I'm comfortable talking with Peter. I know him from another small project we worked on together when I was on the customer escalation team, and I already have an appointment scheduled with him right after lunch," I answered. "He's a pretty fair guy, and I think he'll listen to my opinion, even though he's made some decisions that I didn't agree with because I thought they had a negative impact on the customer. I'd really like to understand what went into those decisions. He seems pretty detail-oriented, so maybe I should go to the meeting with him armed with information about the last few weeks' results. Maria from Marketing could probably help pull some of that information from system reports before the meeting."

Getting Organized

"These ideas sound like they'd work as a good start," Stephanie said. "Shall we make them into action items from our meeting? Why don't you record them in your journal?"

"Sounds good to me," I said as I jotted them down.

- *Lunch with new supervisory team.*

- *Pull campaign results to date.*

- *Jot down innovative techniques used to sell products.*

"Well, it looks like you've got a good start," Stephanie said. "And just in time. I've got just a few minutes to get ready for a presentation I'm making to Human Resources about the mentor project I'm leading. And just to let you in on a secret, I've got a few butterflies myself, so know that all of us are continually learning and growing our skills!"

She paused and then said, "Before we wrap up, I have some questions for you to think about for our meeting tomorrow. You can put the answers in your journal, and I'd like to begin all of our coaching conversations with them. They'll help us both stay on track and stay focused on what's most critical to be working on." Stephanie handed me a laminated sheet of paper:

- *What have I accomplished since our last meeting?*
- *What didn't I get done but intended to?*
- *The challenges and problems I am facing now…*
- *The opportunity that is available to me right now…*
- *I want to use my coaching time to…*
- *What I commit to doing before the next meeting…*

"I look forward to hearing how the meeting with your new peers went. I'll see you tomorrow—same time, same place," she smiled and ended our session.

As I left Stephanie's office, I felt relieved to have a plan. On my walk back to my desk, I thought to myself how critical this first meeting would be in building rapport and fitting into the supervisory team. I hoped I wouldn't be overstepping my bounds. "Oh well," I said under my breath, "better to do something than nothing at all."

3

Building Rapport with My Peers

I was really looking forward to lunch, and then I remembered that this would be the first time I would see Tiko since my interview. He had asked some tough questions and indicated some concerns because I had no previous management experience. I made a mental note to set up some time with him afterward to let him know that I would be open to his feedback if he thought I was letting the team down. Maybe he could even offer me some tips on what I could do to be a better supervisor.

Getting Off on the Right Foot

I thought about the six teammates I was about to have lunch with. I knew they were all under quite a bit of stress trying to meet sales goals. As we began to eat lunch, I asked how they saw my roles and responsibilities as a member of their team, and what major issues we had in front of us to solve. Natasha and Holly were quick to respond that they were hoping I could help them coach their team members on the techniques I had successfully used to get customers to buy more products and services. They mentioned several individuals who were not selling up to par, and suggested that I should also work with *their* staff members.

What a compliment! But, I had definite concerns that Natasha herself did not know how to sell and so she found it difficult to coach her employees. I wondered how I could, or even *should*, do her work for her. I knew she was doing anything she could to improve her results, since her team was the lowest in sales across the board, and I had heard she was on a performance warning. I wasn't sure that the rumor was accurate, since I really didn't know Natasha very well. I would need to ask her and make sure I had the facts.

"I'd love the opportunity to share everything that I know works," I said. "But I don't know if I'll have the time to work with everyone. Is there a way that we can work together, so we're all up to speed, and then any one of us can do some mini-refreshers? I'd be willing to get some of what works on paper and share it with everyone, as long as everyone is willing to get down and dirty taking calls, and listening to others take calls. I know that I was always impressed when supervisors took calls every week, so they were more in tune to what was happening. Could that work?"

I held my breath. Troy jumped in. "I really like how this idea worked when we decided how to communicate the new performance policy," he said. "It seemed like each of us had a different perspective, and different ideas, but when we each owned pieces of it and then worked and critiqued it together, we all could live with our plan. We had a solid process that worked very smoothly. I vote we take Chris's offer and then, as a group, tweak it so it'll work for all of us."

"That worked *then*, but we really don't have as much time to do it that way *now*," Natasha retorted. "We all have more direct reports since the last reorganization, and I, for one, don't think I have much to offer. You all know that my neck is on the line. I don't even know if I'll have a job next week." The tension in the air became very thick.

I thought quickly, and said, "Natasha, I could start writing down some of the tips that have worked for me, and then work with a few members from each of our teams to test how they work. You could make sure the tips are realistic and clearly explained, I could make the revisions, and then both of us could present them to the others. That would show that you're really trying, and maybe we can focus on one or two of your higher performers that need just a little support and will rally for you. Would that help?"

Setting the Climate with Peers

I held my breath again. This seemed to be one of those make it or break it moments, and Natasha was not predictable.

"Well," she paused, "all right, as long as we can do it on Wednesday afternoon—when I have fewer team members here and before the new hire class gets out on Thursday. I suppose I'd better do something, or I'm going to really be in trouble."

I looked around at the rest of the team and sensed that *everyone* had been holding their breath. I felt that we may have just turned a corner by coming up with a plan, breaking down a few barriers and arriving at a win-win solution. I suddenly realized that the E + R = O formula I learned earlier from Stephanie really worked! One of my outcomes was that I really wanted to share what worked for me, so more of us could experience success, and I also wanted to support a team effort. By responding to concerns and listening to what was needed to have everyone get something out of this solution, it seemed that my response, the "R" in the equation, had been automatically programmed for me. I could hardly wait to let Stephanie know that it worked!

David finished drinking his coffee and then said, "I really would like to spend time coaching my folks on the new product positioning, but my time is being spent pulling reports for everyone since we've lost Matt to another department. I really wonder if anyone looks at them, and it's really bogging me down. Chris, I was hoping you could pick up some of the reporting responsibilities, so I can focus time and energy on my staff's development needs. Think about it, and let me know if you can work with me sometime next week."

Hmm…I knew that reporting was one area I definitely did not understand, so this could be a good opportunity to learn something new, and give David a hand. "David," I said, "I would really like to learn more about reports and give you a hand. I'll let you know after I meet with Peter to see if this could be part of my development objectives."

We then talked about the upcoming employee satisfaction survey, wondering what our associates would say, especially with the added stress they were feeling.

Susan piped up, saying, "Gee, Chris—you just came from the ranks. What do you think everyone is saying about us? You know part of our bonus depends on the results of that survey, don't you?" She smiled.

Now this was a tricky situation. I wondered if Susan was concerned for the good of the whole team, or just herself. She was known as a tough supervisor who didn't always communicate specific expectations and then came down hard on those who didn't meet them. But she was also realistic. She expected people to be responsible for their own actions and was not into babysitting for results. And some people seemed to need babysitting. I made a mental note to ask Stephanie what she thought was the best way to approach this situation.

It seemed as if the response I made right now could make or break my relationship with the entire group. So, I took a deep breath and said, "I'm sure we've all got some areas of strength and areas where, as a supervisory team, we can improve. I know I do. My former team already told me during my good-bye lunch that if I was to continue to have their respect I should make sure I communicated what was going on—good and bad. I'm looking for your help with how best to accomplish this. And I'm looking forward to seeing the results. Besides, my nose has been 'to the grindstone' lately making sales. I haven't spent much time listening to what others put down on the survey," I said with a chuckle.

I looked at Susan to see what she might say. She seemed to be thinking and then said, "I don't really see that any of us has enough time, but this might be one place where, if we did it right the first time, we could spend a whole lot less time taking care of misunderstandings. I just don't want this to turn into a committee where we take forever to come up with solutions." I thought that Susan was a little abrupt, but what she said made sense. Her style and approach were different from mine. I preferred to take time to get everyone's ideas and then make a decision. But she was right. We all were pressed for time. Maybe our differences in style could play off of each other.

Natasha chimed in, "My team already told me that they gave me high marks in sharing corporate information, but really wanted me to spend more time coaching on specific behaviors during their customer interactions to help them meet their goals." I'm glad Natasha said this, since it confirmed that she was at least aware that she'd been letting coaching time slip. She was known among the ranks for not dealing with her employees, and they seemed to get away with everything.

Holly added with commitment in her voice, "If last year is any indicator, everyone in management will take the results seriously. I'm sure Peter will set up a staff meeting just to create action plans around those areas where we really need to put some focused improvement effort."

"That makes sense," I said. "I remember, Holly, when you were asked to facilitate our team meeting last year. You described the results, told us specifically what all supervisors were focusing on, and then what your individual goal was. I remember you saying that you expected us to help you stay accountable to your goal of meeting with each of us at least one hour per month to discuss our development goals, and areas where we could focus our sales efforts."

"Yeah, we mean well," Susan replied, "but the problem here is there is no consequence for those individuals who don't take personal responsibility. It seems like accountability is just on paper rather than acted on around here."

Susan had a point, but I wasn't sure everyone agreed. I could already see a few eyes roll.

Holly quickly jumped back in. "Susan, I don't disagree with you," she said. "I've struggled with how to hold my staff accountable. I think it really starts with us, by making sure we have met with each individual agent and set up specific goals. Like Chris said, after I made that announcement last year, the whole team was relentless! The good news is that I met my goal, and Chris is a good example of what those one-on-ones produced!" I made a note to myself to remember that this was a best practice, and to set goals with my new team.

The waiter laid each of our checks on the table. I looked at my watch, and said, "Wow, time sure flies when we get going. I really appreciate being welcomed to the team. I hope we can have lunch often to see where we can work together."

David stood up. "Speaking of goals, I need to get to those reports. Chris, I can show you how to look at the reports, and how we fill in the information for Peter. Let me know when you've got a half-hour free."

With that, everyone stood up and gathered their things.

Motivating Team Members to Play on the Same Team

Tiko had been very quiet throughout the meal, and I could tell that he wasn't really thrilled by this discussion. I knew he wanted someone else to get the supervisor job, and it looked like he was going to give me a hard time. As I got up to go, I said, "Hey, Tiko. Can I walk back to the office with you?"

Tiko's eyebrows rose. "Sure. I've got just a few minutes before I have to take my turn on the Scheduling Desk," he said.

I swallowed, feeling my hands get a little sweaty. "Well, I just wanted to make sure I let you know that I really appreciated the questions you asked in my interview," I said. "I know that I wasn't your first choice, but I really respect your opinion and what you've been able to accomplish with your team. I hope that you'll be willing to tell me if you see that I'm on the wrong path. I'm sure I could learn a lot from you."

Tiko's face was a bit red. I hoped I hadn't embarrassed him. "Chris, I didn't realize I was such an open book," he replied. "I *did* think we could have used someone with more management experience, but I see now that you have many leadership qualities. I'm concerned that we don't manage to our numbers very well and was hoping we would hire someone with experience doing that. I guess we'll figure it out. As long as the feedback goes both ways, I'd be glad to buddy up with you and share observations. I know we both have a lot to learn. I better get going though, or I'll be on the hot seat with Tim, who's staffing the desk right now."

"Thanks, Tiko. We'll talk again soon," I said.

"Whew, that seemed to go pretty well," I mumbled to myself. I remembered a favorite quotation from a research paper I had done on Henry Ford that always stayed with me:

"A setback is the opportunity to begin again more intelligently."

I didn't want to forget any of my action items or lessons learned, plus I knew that I needed to keep my promises in order to gain respect from my new fellow supervisors. When I got back to my desk, I pulled out my journal, and wrote:

- *Ask Stephanie about babysitting vs. accountability.*
- *Ask David how to prepare reporting information.*
- *Ask Peter how to use the report summary.*
- *Arrange time with Tiko to get feedback.*
- *Write out Cheat Sheet and set time to meet with Natasha.*
- *Set goals with each of my team members.*
- *Consider how to communicate results based on employee survey.*
- *Dealing with uncomfortable issues quickly takes less energy.*

I wanted to get a summary of data from our campaign results before my meeting with Peter. I knew I had last week's revenue results in an e-mail, but I didn't know how to integrate the phone statistics, quality results, customer satisfaction, and sales goals results from the computer system. I just knew that all the phone agents were stressed from the unusually high number of calls, mostly about new products. I remembered that Maria, our statistics guru, had once explained this to our new hire class, and was the respected voice when it came to reports, so I walked by her desk to see if she could give me a quick overview on how to pull the information I was looking for.

As I came to Maria's desk, she looked up. "Hi, Chris. Congratulations on your new position! What's up?"

Understanding Reports

"Thanks," I said, "I'm very excited about the new job, and in fact that's why I stopped by. Do you have a few minutes to show me how to pull statistics from the system for last week? I'd like to see how we're doing with our service level, and how we scored on quality over the last 30 days."

"Sure…," Maria said tentatively. "You know it's been a little crazy around here with the training and new products introduced, and I don't have to tell you that we've all been swamped. I can spare about 30 minutes before I need to pull end of quarter results and I'm compiling our new customer survey results, which will take me the rest of the day," she said, rolling her eyes. "It'd be faster if I just pull the reports this time, and we can make an appointment when I have more time to show you how to do it yourself. In fact, it will be perfect timing to show you how quality, sales and customer satisfaction correlate with each other."

I was a little disappointed, but didn't want to burn this important bridge either. "If this is not a good time, I can come back later, Maria," I said.

"No, it'll just take a few minutes, really, and the more people who know how to run and analyze these reports, the better we can all manage what's happening each day," she said. She seemed to push just a few keys on her computer, grabbed a handful of sheets off the printer and then turned around. "These will give you some preliminary data," Maria continued, "but the most important thing to know is what you're going to do with the numbers you're pulling. There is so much information in the system that it can be overwhelming at first. So what are you trying to figure out?"

I explained that I thought the new marketing campaign was being well received by our customers, but that the agents were getting overwhelmed with the number of calls always in queue, and that I wasn't convinced we'd scheduled enough time for the agents to ask questions after the initial training. I also wondered how our revenue goals were stacking up against our call volume, and if we were still maintaining our base quality standards. "Finally," I said, "I don't think agents really understand how the call center works, especially when we're this busy, and I know they don't understand how everyone impacts the bottom line.

"I was thinking I would use this information at a meeting I have with Peter and see if he's open to talking about it during our supervisory meeting," I continued. "And I'd like to understand how we actually do the scheduling so I can understand it. My gut feeling is that we're not staffed to handle all of the calls and e-mails we're getting."

Maria's eyes lit up. "Chris, I love the numbers game with reports, and especially how helpful they can be when we analyze them and understand what they tell us," she said. "The thing to remember about reports is that you need to keep them simple. The computer is set up to do most of the calculations, but we have to know how to apply the information. This first chart gives specific information about efficiencies on the phone. The important question is whether the reps are spending their time talking to our customers. For example, look at this chart," she said as she showed me the first page:

% on Phone	Employee Name	Logged in Time	Talk Time	Wait Time	Other Time
57%	Esi	8:00:12	4:32:15	2:52	30:0
28%	Ty	6:50:00	2:14:52	1:32	45:0
19%	Gerry	4:00:30	1:30:37	2:45	55:0
85%	Joanne	8:00:20	6:50:18	:30	

"An associate works 8 hours a day, Maria began. "It isn't feasible for them to talk 100% of the time. Within the 8 hours, we determine how many hours the associate is expected to talk to customers. In this chart, you see that Joanne was on calls 85% of the time, which is our goal. Esi, Ty and Gerry were substantially under goal. However, we can't make any assumptions just from the data. For example, I know that Esi, Ty and Gerry have been working with the new hire class.

"Let's say the average for our call center associates to be talking to customers changes to 90%," she said. "In an 8-hour day, an associate has two 15-minute breaks. So the 90% average is calculated on 7.5 hours. This means that the talk time for the day should be 6 hours and 45 minutes."

She drew a breath and smiled to reassure me. "To gain efficiencies in a call center, one of the main things to look at is whether the associates are spending time doing the right thing," she explained. "When this type of reporting is first done, most supervisors are very surprised as there are always a couple of people who are not doing what they are expected to do. They can often lead you to believe they are working diligently, so it is critical to have factual data. The data provides backup for supervisory action. Without accountability in place, the best efficiencies will not be reached."

Then Maria pulled a piece of paper from the pile. "This first report shows the volume of calls coming in and at what time of the day. Our center takes calls from many different time zones, so the number of calls varies at all hours of the day," she explained. "We often aren't busy at the start of the day because most of our customers are opening their own businesses, but we get very busy toward the end of the day when they are trying to finish up before going home. Calls also vary depending on the day of the week. For example, we are much busier on Monday than on Friday."

"There are a few ways to look at our phone traffic," Maria explained. "Our Automated Call Distribution, or ACD, unit gives us the data on a second report that tells us the time calls have arrived in our center. The downfall to using just this process is that you are dependent on the customer to give you the data. They often press the wrong prompt in the ACD, resulting in inaccurate data. We also generate a third report to look at the work actually keyed into the system, and at what time it is keyed. This gives us a way to cross-reference call data with transactions. However, we can't use this report alone, because it doesn't include our service calls. We are just now completing a 'call qualifying report', which is another way to look at phone traffic. Management, with the help of staff, determines reasons for each call, assigns a code and then associates key the code after each call. This will help us look at various call volumes to allow us to better manage our staffing.

"Now," she said, "this next report pulls much of this data together. Our management team has identified five types of calls that we take in our call center." Maria showed me this report:

Call Qualifying Report*

Average Minutes per Call	5	4	6	1	2		
Hour of the Day	# Call type 1	# Call type 2	# Call type 3	# Call type 4	# Call type 5	Required Minutes Needed	# Associates Needed
8	8	6	15	4	8	174	3.87
9	18	25	27	28	35	450	10.00
10	15	19	29	27	34	420	9.33
11	25	10	16	21	24	330	7.33
12	29	18	22	25	24	422	9.38
13	25	35	50	22	15	617	13.71
14	50	22	26	28	32	586	13.02
15	35	29	33	27	19	554	12.31
16	21	25	26	29	35	460	10.22
17	28	28	22	26	28	466	10.36
18	25	20	20	35	24	408	9.07
19	35	29	29	31	31	558	12.40
20	15	14	12	19	21	264	5.87
	329	280	327	322	330	5709	

*This assumes each associate works about 45 minutes in each hour.

I jumped in. "Maria, it's amazing how you keep all these reports straight and what valuable information they provide if you know what you're looking for," I said. I was still a bit puzzled though. "I see here that we may only need one or two associates during the first hour of the morning, and then we quickly need more associates. With 8-hour shifts, what do the others do when calls aren't coming in?"

"Interesting question, Chris," said Maria. "There are other factors that determine scheduling. We use a tool called workforce management. It helps us to schedule employees based on call volume, break schedules, after-call work, and other necessary tasks that are non-phone-related. It is important to understand the base that workforce management uses. Once the numbers are plugged in, you need to go back to see if it, indeed, resembles reality. For example, does call type #1 *really* take 5 minutes on average for the associate to manage?" she continued. "Workforce management figures out the time required on the phones and the associates' schedule. But, the supervisor needs to understand how long calls take to make sure that the calls are being managed efficiently."

"When doing this analysis, there is also a philosophical issue to keep in mind—how fast we want to answer our phones," Maria explained. "For example, our existing standards require that 80% of the calls be answered in 20 seconds or less. Currently, that meets our business needs and is satisfying to our customers. At one point in time, we answered 90% of calls in 20 seconds or less. We changed because we gained very little in terms of customer satisfaction, but created a lot of employee stress."

"We are improving our ability to take advantage of down time at different intervals," she continued. "For example, we've had some of our associates make callbacks to customers for quality checks, we've scheduled training, and we're providing backup support for billing."

"Maria, this is beginning to make sense to me, but I still don't know if we are adequately staffed," I said.

"From what I've seen, Chris, we are adequately staffed for our current service calls. However, as we've put more emphasis on up-selling, I think our average call time has increased significantly," Maria replied. "I'm actually working on the critical next step, which is to compare average call time vs. schedule time with sales completed, so we have factual data to argue for more staffing."

"Hmmm, this is all very interesting," I said. "May I keep these to look over?"

"Sure," Maria replied. "I just pulled some of the high-level data for you. There's much more detail available, but I think this will give you a good start for your meeting with Peter. And always remember that numbers are only indicators of what is happening; you need to view them in the context of what is going on in the business, our staff, and our supervisory team. Use them to formulate the questions that will answer the cause and effect to point you in the right direction."

"I see I have a lot to learn," I sighed.

"Chris, just take one step at a time," she said. "It will begin to make sense to you as you compare the data over time. I'd be happy to answer your questions, and work with you more, but right now I really need to get back to work. I will get some additional reports to you which will include our revenue per contact, items per order, and our overall revenue this year compared to last year."

"Thanks so much for your time, Maria. I'm sure I'll have many more questions, but I know you need to get back to work," I continued. "I'll send you an e-mail with some options for a meeting with you so you can show me how to pull the reports myself."

"Good idea. Let me know if you need anything else in the meantime," Maria replied and then turned back to her computer.

This all was a little bit overwhelming, but I hoped that if I just studied, the reports would make sense. And I sure was glad there were all of these experts around to help me.

4

Learning About Team Ground Rules

The butterflies were back. I had worked with Peter before, but somehow this felt different. I really wanted to do some positive things in the organization, and I had *so* many ideas. I remembered Stephanie's advice and thumbed through my journal, noting that I wanted to cover three items with Peter. As I reviewed them, I started to calm down.

I walked over to Peter's office. His office was known around the call center as "the hub" since it bordered the three major teams in the call center, and it had two huge boards posted with sales results year to date, as well as by the hour. I noticed on the overhead reader board that we had more than 35 calls in queue, but we were well over our revenue goals for the day. I knew that if we kept up this pace we'd exceed our revenue projections, but agents and supervisors were going to burn out, and our absenteeism and attrition would skyrocket. We were just entering our true peak period, so that could be disastrous, leaving no wiggle room for overflow calls.

I knocked on Peter's door. He had stacks of folders on his floor and desk, with several call back messages sitting near his phone. He closed his e-mail, stood up, shook my hand, and said, "Chris, it's sure wonderful to have you on board. I'm looking forward to all you can offer our team and company."

"Thanks, Peter," I said, feeling a little calmer. "I'm really glad to be here. And I know you're really busy, and we've got calls in queue." I winced and said, "I almost want to jump on the phone to alleviate the wait time."

Peter nodded. "I know how you feel. It is important that you and I have a few minutes together before the team meeting, and besides, one of our jobs is to ensure we're staffed properly so we don't need to all be on the phones," he said. "This new campaign has created more volume than we predicted. But it's a problem I don't mind having to deal with." He chuckled, and then continued. "Chris, I'm really pleased that you accepted the new supervisor position. I have a feeling that our whole team will be spending more time together as we figure out how to get everything done, work with these new customers, and reach our revenue goals. Your background and skills with customers are real assets to our supervisory team. So, what's on your mind?"

I took a deep breath. "Well, I'm wondering what I should do to be prepared for our team meeting tomorrow morning? I had lunch with the other supervisors today, and I know we're all anxious about the employee satisfaction results. I am also concerned about our aggressive revenue goals and all of the new campaigns coming at us. I don't think we're really prepared to handle all of this at once," I continued firmly. "And I wanted to talk with you about my own development plans."

Team Dynamics and Ground Rules

Peter nodded his head in understanding. "I see that it hasn't taken you long to recognize the challenges we're facing right now. I'm confident that with our team, and now your help, we can meet our revenue goals and not burn everyone out. In fact, that very discussion is a part of our supervisory team agenda. Let me show you the rest of the agenda we have for tomorrow's meeting."

As he swiveled his chair back to his computer, he said, "I send out the agenda the day before the meeting so everyone arrives prepared to discuss the topics. I'll add you to my distribution list so you'll get them from now on. I believe that meetings are more productive when everyone does their 'homework' first, and we spend our time together problem solving. However, I also leave time for what I call 'open microphone', so everyone has a chance to bring up other issues that need our attention. We're also going to have a half-day offsite team-building session at the end of the month. This will be especially helpful to you as a new supervisor since all of our roles are shifting a bit. There we'll discuss our employee and customer satisfaction results to determine individual and team action plans."

As he printed out the agenda, I pulled out the reports I had put together. I also pulled out the Cheat Sheet I had put together a few weeks ago to help me remember all the new products and services of this latest campaign, including features, how they benefited the customer, and some of my favorite questions to ask customers that seemed to put them at ease and give me the information I needed to provide quality service.

Peter handed me the agenda. As I glanced at it, I saw that my concerns were already on the agenda! I was relieved, excited and more determined than ever to really make a difference on this team.

Team Meeting Agenda

Accomplishments Since Last Meeting	*10 min*
Marketing Campaigns and Revenue Goals	
Questions on Update	*5 min*
Issues and Discussion	*15 min*
Training Needs for New Products	*15 min*
Prep for Team Building	*5 min*
Open Microphone	*25 min*
Review of Action Items	*10 min*
Meeting Process	*5 min*

He handed me another sheet of paper. "I have a few ground rules that help us stay on task, but also allow for important discussions in how we run our business," he said. "Let me review them with you, since everyone else knows them already."

Team Meeting Ground Rules

- *Start on Time*
- *Encourage Questions*
- *Give Everyone Air Time*
- *Strive for Excellence, Not Perfection*

- *Maintain Confidentiality*

- *Check Process at End of Meeting*

- *End on Time*

- *Respect Differences of Opinion*

- *Listen Carefully*

- *Accept Group Accountability*

"I think starting on time and ending on time is pretty clear," Peter continued. "Everyone's time is valuable, and when we are late, it's disrespectful as well as inefficient. I find when we really listen carefully, we make sure we ask questions to clarify what someone's intention is rather than jump to conclusions or make judgments. I've also discovered when we truly understand someone's point of view, we gain insight into other angles of accomplishing the same goal. Often, this creates a win-win outcome as we build on each other's ideas. Respecting differences of opinion, of course, goes hand in hand with listening. Sometimes we agree to disagree; however, my experience is that when we have respect for one another's ideas, we foster honesty with each other that is essential to meet our goals."

Peter paused. "Does this make sense to you so far?" he asked.

I was feeling more encouraged by the minute and knew that I had made the right decision to accept this position. "Yes," I replied. "In fact, this really helps me understand how I can fit more easily into the group. I have lots of ideas that I would like to share. And this also gives me some ideas about running my own team meetings."

"I never knew about the importance of team ground rules until I had a group with an impossible deadline, and many differences of opinions on how to accomplish the goal. We had established ground rules, but never really used them until that day. When not one person was listening to the other except to refute the point, we called a time out, and reviewed the ground rules to 'Listen carefully' and 'Respect differences of opinion.' It made a difference in the whole atmosphere of getting the job done, so much so that we not only beat the deadline, but came in under budget as well!"

Quoted by a Manager of a 200-seat call center

Achieving Buy-In

"Terrific," Peter said with a smile. "We need all your ideas, and I'd like to see more of our supervisors adapt these standards for their team meetings. Since you are the one with the most recent experience on the floor, your opinion will go a long way toward making sure our solutions are realistic and will get us what we want."

Grinning, I said, "Well, I actually was wondering how I could share two ideas in this team meeting." I paused to think how I could communicate my thoughts clearly.

"I understand that our company is in a major transition right now, and I've read all the memos about our shareholders wanting us to gain market share," I explained. "I think we'd reach this long-term goal if we slowed down and did it right from the start." Peter looked interested. I took a deep breath. "I think our goals are a bit too aggressive for the first month. Maria printed some basic reports and confirmed what I thought I saw happening last week." I handed him what Maria and I had pulled from the system.

"If I understand how Maria explained these to me," I continued, "then we've actually increased our average handle time by about 2 minutes on average, and our service level is suffering. However, we also had more than 8% of our workforce out last week but were still able to achieve a 4% increase in revenue over the prior week. I think it's amazing." I paused to check his reaction. He continued to nod, and said, "Go on."

"I know that everyone on the floor wants us to reach, and even exceed, our goals," I said, "but I'm concerned that our aggressiveness is burning people out, and we'll see more and more absences. I think if we slightly adjusted our goals we would keep our agents working hard, but not destroy morale."

"Chris, you have a point," Peter remarked. "Our challenge is not only to balance the workload, but also to meet our shareholders' objectives. Upper management has given us the parameters to work within, and they hold me accountable to get the results within or under budget. I'm afraid adjusting our goals isn't an option. But we can discuss your ideas further during the team meeting and see what the others think, and come up with potential solutions so we don't burn folks out."

"I know I have a lot to learn," I said, and took another deep breath. "But I think if we created some mini-training sessions on positioning our new products, we'd have better results all the way around. I think that will help us handle calls more confidently and efficiently. I don't believe that everyone has their ear tuned into the customer, causing us to miss sales opportunities and leave money on the table." I continued, "I also don't think many folks understand how the calls are routed, or how the after call work, or ACW, buttons should be used, so I don't think we're capturing the data we need to make staffing decisions." I paused, and then said, "I have so many more ideas I'd like us to try. I'm also putting together this Cheat Sheet about the benefits of our new products that I thought I could share with everyone…if you'd like," I said hesitantly.

Speaking Our Truths

Phew! It was said. It felt good to be able to say what was on my mind and have someone help me focus on solutions.

"You're absolutely right," Peter replied. "We have asked everyone to absorb quite a bit of information in a short period of time. I'd like to see what you've come up with regarding tips to make sure they align with our values and mission."

Peter reviewed the reports, and said with a twinkle in his eye, "It's wonderful you've started to learn how to use these reports. Make copies for the meeting and I'll include this in the update on our campaigns and revenue goals; the impact on our staff is a critical factor in our success. A good time to share your ideas is during the 'open microphone' portion of the meeting," he continued. "Think about just one or two of your best ones so the group isn't overwhelmed. This will also give them a chance to contribute some of their ideas. I've found that when everyone has a part in creating the solution, they'll buy into it and actually give it a real try. When forced upon them, they'll spit it out before they even taste it!"

I would have to remember to write this valuable insight into my journal. I had learned at least one way to be diplomatic about what I really thought without coming off as a know-it-all.

"Learning how to read and use reports, or creating a Cheat Sheet, are both examples of personal accountability," Peter continued, "which leads me to the next ground rule, group accountability. By understanding the impact of our decisions and behaviors on the whole business, we can put a priority on excellence while supporting each other in what needs to be accomplished."

"This whole issue of accountability has me worried," I said. "I'm going to bring this up the next time I meet with my coach, Stephanie, to figure out how to get my new team to be accountable, but I also don't want to alienate them."

"Our whole staff is struggling with this," Peter replied. "I'm thinking of having a training session on goal setting. I'd be interested to know what you come up with in your conversations with Stephanie. I'm glad you're working with her since, with all of our new products and sales goals, I really haven't had a chance to spend time developing everyone the way I'd like to."

I thought a minute and said, "Well, I'd be happy to help in any way I can. I'll let you know about any insights I gain from my work with Stephanie."

A worry that I hadn't thought of before suddenly struck me. Before I could contain myself, I blurted out, "What happens if we agree to a solution, and then we all don't stick with it, or give it a real chance?"

"Hmmm, that's a tough one," he said. Peter wrinkled his brow and then continued, "I think this is where the ground rule of 'air time for everyone' plays a part. For example, you could put your concern on the table by asking the group how we should give each other feedback when we don't think everyone's on board or staying committed to the solution. Then, as facilitator of the meeting, I make sure everyone has their say before we come to an agreed-upon solution. If we respect each other and follow our rule of confidentiality—where we agree that anything that is said in the meeting stays in the meeting and is not repeated—then my experience is that individuals will usually say what's on their mind. Then we all have a better understanding of how we can support someone who is not following the process. The bottom line is that it is my job to handle a team member that does not follow the group goals. I need to hold them accountable, but I will not discuss their lack of follow-through with the group. I'm sure if I had an issue that I was working on with you, for example, you would not want me to talk about it with the group."

I nodded in agreement.

"Realize, too," Peter added, "that sometimes the very person who appears cautious or uncommitted may see an issue or have another concern we hadn't initially thought about, that could actually take us backward instead of forward. It's then that one of us asks the difficult question, positioned in a non-threatening way, something like, 'I noticed that all of us aren't having as much success trying *x*. I'd like us to talk about what's working and not working for each of us.' And remember," he laughed, "all questions are fair game."

I realized that dealing with team issues in a diplomatic way was going to be a new experience for me—something I was really going to have to work on. I'd have to put this idea in my journal as well.

Peter kept talking, and I eagerly listened. "I asked the group to include the ground rule that we strive for excellence rather than perfection," he said. "I was once part of a team that discussed ideas to death, trying to anticipate every possible reason why the solution wouldn't work. They either talked themselves out of most of their ideas or became so paralyzed that they never really made any progress. I don't want to lead a team where this happens."

I grinned. "I often do the opposite and usually jump in with both feet first before I've thought of all the consequences," I said.

Plus/Delta Process

Peter stroked his chin. "Well then, I think our process check at the end of the meeting will help you. We ask each other, and write on a flipchart, what we thought went well in our meeting that we'd want to continue including, as well as what we'd like to change or do differently the next time so we continually strive to work together as a cohesive group, and what support we can offer one another," he explained. "I call it a 'Plus/Delta' process check. Notice the word *delta*, which is the Greek word for 'change'. For example, here is the Plus/Delta from our last meeting."

He pulled out a flipchart paper from behind his desk. It looked like this:

> *PLUS*
> *Good discussion about staffing.*
> *Everyone had a chance to share.*
>
>
> *DELTA*
> *Look at reports, adjusting for next month.*
> *Come prepared with data.*

"In fact," Peter explained, "many of the team leaders are using it as part of their team meetings. We usually keep track of these and sometimes review them in case we see ourselves slipping into old habits."

"This is definitely a different way to think about what we don't like, and feels like a safer way to talk about the negative," I said. "I'm looking forward to seeing it in action."

Peter looked at his wall clock. "Chris, our appointment time is just about up. Before you go, let's agree to a standing check-in every day. I usually like to do a quick 10-minute team huddle before the start of each shift, so I can communicate any urgent messages, and just check in to see how things are going," he said. "I like to make sure I'm staying in touch with everyone in between team meetings. And of course, you can always make an appointment for additional time if you need it."

We agreed to meet every Tuesday at 1 p.m. and I shook Peter's hand.

"I'm glad I landed on your team, Peter," I said. "I know I'll learn a lot just by watching you in action, and I'm going to bring my journal the next time to keep track of everything I'm learning!"

Peter laughed. "Stephanie is a wonderful coach," he said. "Sometimes I take out my journal from my first year and read through it. I'm often amazed at how much of what I learned from her I still use today. She'll give you a solid foundation to take with you wherever you go. I even use some of my learning at home, too!"

I grinned back at Peter. "Thanks for getting me ready for the team meeting. I'll see you in the morning, ready to share my ideas!"

I returned to my desk, pulled out my journal, and added to my list of items to remember:

- *Get buy-in by sharing 1-2 ideas, inviting others to share.*

- *If someone isn't doing what we agreed upon, ask them about it rather than getting frustrated. They may see a stone in the path that no one else sees.*

- *All questions are fair game.*

- *Use Plus/Delta process for meeting evaluation.*

- *Ask Stephanie how to deal with issues diplomatically.*

5

Balancing Work and Family Life

As I closed my journal, I looked at my watch. I had only about an hour left in the day, so I decided to stay late and work more on the Cheat Sheet to help the associates sell products from the marketing campaign. I wanted to have a draft ready to show the other supervisors at tomorrow's meeting so we could get a jump start on finalizing and using the Cheat Sheet. The more quickly we could get tools into the hands of the associates, the better we'd be able to handle our volume, reach our revenue goals, *and* keep morale high.

I pulled out a folder where I'd stashed all the scrap pieces of paper from my old desk. I always wrote down ideas, questions and points to remember while on calls with customers. How could I organize this collage of ideas so it would be useful for others?

Creating the Cheat Sheet

I thought back to conversations I'd had with customers. The first step was to make certain I understood their business, and then determine what Power Solutions service or product would best help them accomplish their goals, usually saving time or money. My eye caught the worn edge of a handout from a training class that listed the products and services and their features. I realized that most of my scribbles were questions I used to identify customer needs and solutions.

After looking at the questions for a few minutes, I decided to organize these issues into columns.

I labeled the first column "Customer Needs". Why did our best customers typically use our products and services and what problems did those products address and/or solve? I wrote down some of the common phrases I'd heard customers use. Then I drew a line for the next column and jotted down my favorite questions that uncovered what was important to the customer. I was getting excited as this started coming together.

I knew that I often positioned product features differently than other associates I had worked with. I always tried to match "pain points" or needs voiced by customers to specific features and benefits of our products and services. So, I drew a fourth column and wrote down a few features and benefits I often discussed with customers. After a few more minutes, I sat back and looked at how the sheet was shaping up.

Something was still missing. How could I *show* agents how to match customer needs to products? I had always done it so naturally on the phone.

Replaying a few conversations in my mind, I remembered one of my first lessons when I started taking calls. I had to really listen to customers and remain *very* focused on what was being said. When I heard a problem that I thought one of our products or services could solve, I jotted it down on my note paper. By matching the customer need to the product benefit, I could think about a solution. In this way I helped solve the customer problem instead of merely pushing for a sale. So I quickly inserted a new column and noted concerns I often heard from customers.

I sat back and took a look at it again.

Customer Needs	Questions to Ask	Customer Concerns	Product Solutions
Easy way to keep track of inventory and re-order parts	How do you usually know when you need to re-order parts?	• Inventory is difficult to track • Customers must frequently wait for parts • Lose business because parts are not available	Inventory Scanner: • Bar code automatically scanned at cash register • Daily report for parts sold and those to be re-stocked • Set own parameters for restocking

Please see Appendix #1 for entire Cheat Sheet.

Learning That I'm Not Perfect

"Looking pretty good for a first stab—time to call it a day," I said to myself, looking at my watch. It was already 6 p.m.! I had spent almost two hours pulling this together, but I felt very encouraged with what I had developed. I noticed that my cell phone was blinking with messages. I had turned the ringer off when I was in the meeting with Peter and had forgotten to turn it back on.

As I listened to the three messages, my stomach began to churn. I remembered I had promised this morning that I would practice with my 13-year-old daughter, Lanie, before her big tryout for the soccer team. She had to be at the tryouts by 6:15. She had left three messages wondering where I was. Her last message told me she was getting a ride with my neighbor. Now, I would barely make it over to the field to watch her tryouts, much less to help her practice. I was in hot water.

I grabbed my coat and practically ran over Stephanie on my way out the door. "Pardon me, Stephanie. I'm really late—and probably in big trouble with my daughter," I gasped. "I got wrapped up in working on the Cheat Sheet for coaching agents and lost track of time. You really have a big job on your hands to help me manage my time! See you tomorrow!"

I drove as fast as I dared, and pulled into the field parking lot. I opened the door as I put the car into park, and then raced over to the group of parents who were watching the tryouts. What explanation would I give my daughter? It was difficult enough living with the unpredictability of a 13-year-old. At home, we always stressed the importance of honoring commitments and follow through and, here I was, demonstrating the exact opposite.

This morning's conversation was just one of several over the last few weeks with Lanie about her interest in joining the soccer team. She was unsure about making the time commitment to the travel team, and she wasn't sure she was good enough to be selected for the position she really liked to play.

I had convinced her that it was a good idea to set high goals—and to learn from the experience of playing with others better than she was—even if it meant sitting on the bench at first. But I'd warned, "Once you make a commitment, you'll need to follow it through, even if you're on the bench the whole season." I used the analogy of applying for and getting my new job. "I decided to challenge myself, learn from others and make a commitment to improve the company results." Although she pretended not to hear me, I knew from her expression that she was at least thinking about it.

She announced at breakfast this morning that she had decided to try out, and then asked me to practice passing skills with her when I got home from work, before driving her to tryouts at the field. I said I'd be home by 5:30, and I promised I'd spend 30 minutes with her before I took her to the tryouts. She was going to warm up and practice by herself until then.

As these thoughts ran through my mind, I walked up to the fence and found my neighbor standing and watching her daughter. I swallowed and said, "Jasmine, thanks for bailing me out and driving Lanie over with you. I lost track of time at work."

"No problem," Jasmine replied. "We were coming over anyway, and the girls practiced and warmed up together before we left. They're both looking really good."

We turned back to watch the girls. I was relieved that Lanie had at least practiced and warmed up. I would make it up to her. I saw the girls going through the paces and looked for Lanie in the lineup. She was tall for her age, so she was easy to spot. She looked confident and was doing a good job of handling the ball. "It took some convincing, but I think this is a good experience for her—kind of like making the first move for a job interview," I said to Jasmine with a chuckle.

"Yeah, I know what you mean. I sure learned quite a bit about taking risks when I applied for a different position at work. I didn't get the job," Jasmine replied candidly, "but I sure learned from the experience. I wouldn't have had the confidence to try for a promotion if I hadn't had other experiences taking risks. I would have been devastated when I got the notice that they'd chosen someone else. But I know from playing sports that it's generally not the last shot that counts, but more what you do going forward. I'm going back to school to get the courses I need, and I'll try again next year."

> *"You gain strength, courage, and confidence by each experience in which you really stop to look fear in the face. You are able to say to yourself, 'I have lived through this horror. I can take the next thing that comes along.' You must do the thing you think you cannot do."*

Eleanor Roosevelt

Jasmine was always pretty intuitive, and I wanted to remember her "words of wisdom" in the event Lanie didn't make the team. When the tryouts ended, the girls left the field and walked over to the group of parents gathered around the fence. Lanie caught my eye and waved good-bye to her friends. As she walked up, she said cheerfully, "Got stuck at work on the new job, huh?"

Wow, she was letting me off pretty easily. "I totally lost track of time," I replied. "I'm sorry I let you down. You looked really good out there."

Lanie smiled sheepishly. "Well, if I make the team, I'll need a lot more practice, so you're not off the hook yet!" She continued, teasing, "And of course I'll need new shoes. I'm starving. What's for dinner?"

Whew! Thank goodness for my teenager's ability to rebound so quickly. What a day! I felt exhausted and could hardly wait for bedtime.

6

Meeting Facilitation in Action

I had tossed and turned all night, thinking about the day ahead and how I was going to better manage my time. I knew that when I became absorbed in a project, I had a tendency to completely lose track of everything around me. Maybe Coach Stephanie would have a cure for me. I resolved to go home on time today, too!

I walked to the copy machine to quickly make some copies of the Cheat Sheet I had finished last night. The machine was out of paper, so I had to hunt down the key to the supply room to get more. I finally found the key and refilled the machine's paper drawer. If I didn't hurry, I was going to be late for the supervisory meeting.

I rushed back to my desk to grab the meeting folder and my journal, and then realized I hadn't written down the meeting room location. This day was going downhill quickly! I looked up Peter's e-mail with the meeting room number and realized I was going to be a few minutes late—not the way to make a good first impression on the whole team!

As I raced over to the conference room, I felt those familiar butterflies again. I awkwardly entered the room with the folder, copies of the Cheat Sheet and my calendar in hand. I was relieved that everyone was still getting settled. The folder had the meeting agenda and ground rules Peter had given me. Tiko waved to me, pointed to an empty chair next to him and said, "Chris, sit down. I want to ask you a question before we get started." I felt the butterflies settle.

Developing Positive Work Relationships

"I just got an e-mail from Human Resources," Tiko said. "They'll have four candidates for us to interview by next week. I have an opening on my team and you have one on yours. What do you say we divide and conquer by interviewing each of them together, and then making our final recommendation to Peter? I think if we interview together, we'll get the finalists hired more quickly, get them more quickly trained, and have an impact on our high call volume. What do you say?"

I thought about it for a minute, and then replied timidly, "I'd really like doing this with you, Tiko, but I've never interviewed or hired anyone in my life."

"Well, you may not have been responsible for making a hiring decision before," Tiko responded, "but you were on the peer selection team last year, and I recall you asked some provocative questions that revealed some of the true colors of the candidates. I can show you some of the questions I usually ask, and you can add your own. How about we do a quick planning session early next week? I think we'd make a dynamic duo. I can share with you how I make hiring decisions, and we can get this process moving!"

I knew that Tiko had a tremendous track record for hiring some of the best associates on the floor. I was certain I could learn quite a few tips from him. "OK, sounds like a good plan," I said. "How does Monday afternoon look for you?"

"OK, 3-5 Monday in my office works perfectly," Tiko answered.

I sighed with relief. I originally thought Tiko was going to be the toughest teammate to get along with, and here he was already reaching out to include me and use my thinking power to benefit the whole team. It sure was worth taking the risk to talk with him earlier!

Just as I finished jotting down the meeting date in my calendar, and a note in my journal to ask Stephanie about interview tips, Peter walked in and called the meeting to order. "I'm sorry I'm late. I've already broken the ground rule about starting meetings on time, but the senior manager meeting went late. Let's get going!" I pulled the agenda from my folder.

Team Meeting Agenda

Accomplishments Since Last Meeting	*10 min*
Marketing Campaigns and Revenue Goals	
Questions on Update	*5 min*
Issues and Discussion	*15 min*
Training Needs for New Products	*15 min*
Prep for Team Building	*5 min*
Open Microphone	*25 min*
Review of Action Items	*10 min*
Meeting Process	*5 min*

Just as Peter had promised, we followed the agenda and honored the timeframe assigned to each topic. I was amazed at the list of accomplishments everyone shared since the last meeting. Susan reported on her liaison role with the workflow development project. I was pleased to learn that the final new product upgrade in our ordering system would be complete by month's end. That sure would make it easier to track orders and fulfillment, as well as keep associates apprised of their sales activity.

Establishing Priorities

David talked about a revised report he was working on to identify shipping errors, with the goal of being more proactive in letting customers know what was happening to their order. Natasha informed us that she had met her personal improvement goal of spending at least one hour with each of her associates during the last week. This was the best news, although I wondered how productive they were. She usually spent most of her time on the floor chitchatting, rather than teaching her staff how to manage customers.

Holly shared that she had been accepted into the coveted MBA program at our local university and would be leaving early on Thursdays. Peter asked us to work offline to share coverage of her team during that time. I hadn't realized that we could go to school on company time. I made a note in my journal to look into this opportunity.

Troy touted that his team met their sales goal for the first time since the latest campaign started, and that he would be cooking breakfast for them on Friday. He invited us to join him if we wanted to come in an hour earlier. We joked with him that we'd have to get a chef's cap, and then we'd have a competition on whose team met goal next. It looked like we'd have a little competition on who was the best breakfast chef, too!

Wow! I sure was a part of an impressive group! I had no idea how much was going on behind the scenes. And I had so many questions I wanted to ask each of them, but those would have to wait.

Peter then brought up several slides on a screen, showing the most current update on revenue goals.

Making Decisions Based on Needs

"Everyone received my e-mail late last night," he said. "To summarize the main points: we've greatly improved over the last two weeks; however we still have a ways to go. We are about 8% off our monthly goal, although we've made significant headway during the last five days. Compared to the first two weeks of the month, we've had a 12% increase in call volume. We were averaging 2.5 items per order. We're still about the same, but the value per order has increased by 35%, so while we're selling the same number of products and services, we're positioning and selling our higher-revenue items, which was a goal we set for ourselves three weeks ago. Congratulations!" The whole team broke out in applause and whistles. It was easy to get caught up in the energy of this group.

Peter continued to the next slide.

"You'll note here," he said, pointing to a graph titled *Call Volume,* "that our call volume has far exceeded our predictions. The good news is that the marketing campaign is taking off like wildfire. The challenge for us all is to think of ways to manage the higher volume without over-stretching our staffing budget. I will be in a better position to make a case to our senior management to increase our staffing budget when we can document consistent and sustained results."

"We do have a new hire class coming out of training next week, which will help alleviate some of the call volume," Peter continued, "and we've had many volunteers sign up to work an extra shift over the next several weeks, which will be covered by our overtime budget. However, we need to continue to search for ways to stay in front of the curve. Does anyone have any other ideas about how we can manage our call volume without damaging the quality of our conversations?"

David piped up. "Peter, I've been thinking about the five associates currently preparing back-end reports," he said. "I don't know if we're making the best use of their time since the data in the system isn't accurate. One short-term solution is to put their project on hold and put them back on the phone until the Technology team tells us the reports are correct." Everyone nodded their heads in agreement.

"That's a good idea," Peter said. "I'd like to share what those associates have discovered so far that could be given to the Technology team. It's important that they see that their work to date is valued and will be used. David, let's talk offline and see what our next steps should be." Then Peter wrote on the board, *Action Items*, and underneath he wrote *David/Peter: Back-End Report Team review.* "Are there any other ideas?" Peter asked.

The group was silent. I decided this was a good time to share my draft Cheat Sheet, since I knew that we could boost efficiency if we handled conversations differently. I jumped in, "As you all know, I agreed to pull together a draft Cheat Sheet detailing what worked for me to increase sales, while meeting average handle time goals. I thought we could refine and pilot it with some of our associates. I think it will give them a leg up on how to handle their calls more competently, as well as help to increase our revenue and manage our call volume. Is this the right time to share the draft?"

"Actually, Chris, that's a perfect segue into our next agenda item, *Training Needs for New Products,*" Peter said. "We discussed at our last meeting several concerns we've been hearing from associates about lacking confidence on how to best position our new products. They've got a pretty good handle on how to sell Power Shelf, which seems to naturally flow when a customer orders product. However, we're 22% below goal for selling the Inventory Scanner and 18% below goal for Power Storage. Let's take a look at what you've come up with."

I handed out the photocopies and described how customer conversations generally developed. I explained the column format, took a deep breath as the team members started to glance over it, and added, "This is just a first stab, but I thought it would get us started." I looked at each of the faces around the table as they continued to read. I couldn't tell from their expressions what they were thinking, so I asked timidly, "What do you think? Will it help us?"

"Chris, this looks like a solid start," Peter responded. "Rather than discuss it right now, I'd like to have you lead a sub-team of two supervisors and two associates to provide additional input, and then put a plan together to test and implement it. We all can filter our feedback through the sub-team. I'll let Shawn from the Scheduling team know that he'll need to arrange for two agents off the phones for approximately two hours next week. I think the sooner we try this, the better for everyone. Are there two volunteers who would like to work with Chris?"

I looked at each of the faces around the table as they looked at their calendars. Natasha glanced up with a gleam in her eye, and said, "Peter, I'd like to make this a priority in my schedule."

"Natasha, that's awesome!" Peter said, smiling. "Who else will join Chris and Natasha?"

Troy raised his hand. "I'd like to help with this project. I need all the help I can get in learning how to coach my group. I'm sure I'll learn a lot just by refining the Cheat Sheet." Chuckling, he continued, "And I have a few members on my team to volunteer as 'guinea pigs'."

Peter nodded, and then turned to the *Action Item* chart and wrote down a second item, *Cheat Sheet: Refine and develop process to implement.* He then turned back to the group and said, "Do you have an idea of when this should be completed?"

I looked at the others. I was anxious to get going on this. "How about we plan to review the next draft at our quarterly planning meeting?" Natasha chimed in. "We'd have time to get a few associates to take a look at it and try it out before then. I think this team needs to feel comfortable with it, too, if everyone is going to really use it." She paused, and looked at Troy and me. "That is, if Troy and Chris can fit it in that soon."

"Natasha, the timing works for me," I replied, "and I agree that we all need to have a final look at it before we bless it. Troy, what's your schedule like?"

"I'm good in a few days, once I get all of my performance reviews done." Troy replied. "Peter, I think we could say by the end of the offsite meeting, we'd have a version ready to go."

"OK then," Peter responded. "Thank you for agreeing to work on this critical project. I'd like you to also involve the Training department so this Cheat Sheet can include any other new products coming up, and so they'll have the final tool to use with the next new-hire classes. Chris, will you take the lead on finding out who from Training should be involved and coordinate with Shawn from Scheduling?"

"Sure," I replied hesitantly. "I'd be glad to. I don't really know who is responsible for Training, but I can go to HR and find out." I made a note on my calendar to call HR first thing in the morning and to leave an e-mail for Shawn to schedule some time to work out the logistics.

The Meeting Facilitator Role

"OK, then," Peter continued. "Let's move on to what you need to do to prep for our team-building meeting. I've scheduled it at Rose's Café from 9 a.m. to 5 p.m. a week from tomorrow. You'll each receive the employee satisfaction results, as well as a team profile questionnaire. I'm hoping Marketing will have last quarter's customer satisfaction results as well, so we can look at the whole picture. I'd like you all to be familiar with your results so we'll be ready to have an in-depth discussion."

He paused. "And be honest with yourselves. This exercise is meant to help us identify our strengths and areas for improvement."

Everyone looked around the table. Susan broke the silence. "I know it was difficult last year for me to hear what my employees *really* thought about what we were doing, but now with some hindsight, they identified many issues that I just didn't want to deal with," she said. "And I remember being shocked that some customers came down so hard on us but, a year later, I can honestly say that our action plan has helped me turn things around with my employees, and the end result is happier customers. I'm looking forward to seeing the results."

"Thanks for that point of view, Susan," Peter replied. "It can sometimes be difficult to hear what others think of us, but we do it to understand what is needed to retain our best employees and to do what's right for our customers. And no matter what, we always need to know how our customers perceive us."

I thought about this. I knew that sometimes customers seemed to want more and more without paying for it, but I hadn't thought about it from this perspective.

Peter continued. "I'll get the satisfaction results to you as soon as I receive them, although I've been told it may be just before our meeting. In any event, we'll use them as part of our discussion," he said.

He paused, looking down at his notes, and said, "Part of our day will also be spent on team-building activities. You'll be receiving a profile questionnaire from HR. You'll need to provide the answers to the questionnaire to Stephanie by Monday. She'll be joining us for part of our team-building session and will use the results to help us understand how we could better work together. I'll have the agenda to you by Tuesday so you can take a look, and I'll include time to review the Cheat Sheet. And," he chuckled, "lunch is on me!"

Peter then pulled a table tent out of his briefcase and stood it in the middle of the table. On each side, it listed the ground rules that he had reviewed with me earlier. He said, "It's now time for open microphone, and here are the ground rules just to remind us to be open to each other's thoughts." He pulled a timer out of his pocket and said, "I'll set the timer for 25 minutes so we can make sure everyone has a chance to contribute if they'd like. Who would like to start?"

I could see that I was working with a real pro when it came to facilitating a meeting. I sat and absorbed how Peter smoothly transitioned the meeting from one topic to another, kept us on time, yet always made it seem as though we had just the right amount of time to complete each agenda item.

My thoughts were interrupted when David began by saying, "I'm really feeling the pressure of getting these reports done every week. I've inherited the responsibility from Matt, and frankly," he said with a shaky voice, "I'm not sure they actually help us manage our business. I think we just keep adding on and adding on and have never taken a step back to see if they're worth the time it takes to pull them together."

I could hear the frustration in his voice and remembered how he asked for help earlier.

"I agree," Holly responded. "There are only two or three areas of information I use, and the rest seems to just pile up on the side of my desk or on the floor."

Tiko piped in and said, "David, the place I worked before coming over to Power Solutions had a terrific process—they called it their Weekly Tally. It had five or six key metrics on it that we had all agreed helped us manage daily operations. As I recall, it had a summary of our quality scores, total revenue, items per order, revenue per call in addition to our occupancy, average handle time, and average speed of answer. I found it very useful, so maybe we could consider something similar here."

"It sounds like we have an issue with reports," Peter interjected. "I sure don't have time to look at all those that I receive either. Those metrics that Tiko mentioned make sense and are similar to the information I look for, but have difficulty locating. We sure have plenty to do without spending time on tasks with no benefit or value. I'd like to see us get a better handle on what the reports are telling us," he continued, "and see if we could create a similar type of reporting tally like Tiko mentioned. I have a feeling that this could tie nicely into our employee and customer satisfaction results, too. Tiko, would you be willing to work with David to draw up a sample?"

Tiko nodded in agreement. "Sure, I'd be delighted to work on anything that will help make this job easier for all of us! David and I can set something up right after this meeting!" he said.

"OK, that was an important issue to discuss," Peter said. "Sometimes we get so wrapped up in what we're doing every day that we don't stop to look at the bigger picture. David, thanks for bringing your concern about reports to the group. I'll include this item on our next agenda, along with your recommendations. We have about seven minutes left for open microphone. Is there anyone else?"

Surfacing Rumors

Susan shifted uncomfortably in her seat. "I don't really know if this is true, but there's a rumor going around that we're going to be buying two smaller service companies. My brother-in-law is a stock broker and asked me about it last night. Is any of it true?" she asked.

Eyebrows raised and everyone gave their full attention to Peter. "I've heard the same rumor, and have a call into Quinn, our VP liaison with corporate, to see what I can find out," he said.

Susan replied sarcastically, "I know we're growing quickly, but it sure would be nice to **not** be the last to know! And I hope they ask us for input this time, rather than just thinking everything automatically fits together," she grumbled.

I remembered how crazy it was when Power Solutions merged with Intricate Parts, Inc. I had just moved to the call center, and it seemed like an eternity before we had their customer information available on our screens. And it was a nightmare following up on order numbers, since we had two separate order entry systems, not to mention the errors that were initially made.

"That was a difficult transition for all of us," Peter said. "I think we learned many valuable lessons to make it go more smoothly this time. And Susan, you were a real help in figuring out solutions to our problems. When I speak with Quinn, I'll make the suggestion that we have representation on the transition team. As soon as I hear something, I'll send out a communication to all of you, and to your teams."

He made a note on his pad and then turned back to the group. "This was an important discussion, and thanks Susan for bringing up your concern. We definitely want to be in front of the rumor mill," Peter added. "You can certainly acknowledge with anyone who asks that we're hearing the same rumor, and as soon as we have the specific details, we'll be communicating them!" The timer buzzed. "We're at the end of our time for open microphone. Let's do our Plus/Delta review process for this meeting."

He went up to the flipchart, and drew a T, writing *Plus* on the left side and *Delta* on the right side. He then asked, "Who has a plus to share?"

"I'd like to commend everyone on getting a lot done during this meeting," Tiko said. "It makes me want to participate more."

"I really appreciate that I have a chance to fix a gap in my own skills by working with Chris on the Cheat Sheet," Natasha said.

"It's good to know how we're going to handle the satisfaction results as a team," Troy chimed in. "I don't feel as vulnerable here as I have in other places."

Peter asked, "Are there any other plusses before we move on to deltas?"

We all shook our heads no, so he continued. "OK, so let's take a look at the deltas, and remember, you can note something negative, but a true delta says what we should *change or do differently* going forward. I'll start by adding, *start meeting on time!*" Everyone laughed, and Peter continued, "I'll have to set the alarm on my watch next time!"

PLUS
What you want to:

- *preserve*

- *continue to do*

- *act on*

DELTA
What you want to:

- *change*

- *strengthen*

- *improve*

- *do differently*

Caution: It's easy to slip into putting negatives, or a minus, instead of a delta. Rather than ignore the negatives, name them, and then think what can be done to make it a positive? Ask the question, what needs to change, improve, or be done differently to create a true delta.

Holly spoke up. "I'm a little uncomfortable about this team profile that we're completing for Stephanie," she said. "I'm not sure what the intent of it is, or if we all will complete it in the way we're supposed to."

"Holly, I understand you're concerned about the intent and process of completing the team profile," Peter replied, "and from the look on everyone's faces, I'm guessing there are others of us with the same question."

We all nodded. "What could we change or do differently to ease your apprehension?" Peter asked.

Holly thought a few moments, and then said, "It would help if Stephanie would e-mail us some information or meet with us to introduce the materials and process, and share what it is all about."

Peter made several notes in the *Delta* column based on what Holly had said. He turned and said, "I'll take ownership of getting this message to Stephanie and let you all know next steps. Are there any more deltas?"

David laughed, and said, "Yeah, we need snacks at these meetings to fuel all this brain power!"

Peter laughed, and added *snacks* to the list. "Okay, I'm noting to bring the first round of snacks to our next team meeting, if you can all stand my cooking!" We all laughed and agreed to take turns for each meeting.

Peter then called the meeting to a close by reminding us of the next one scheduled in two weeks. As I stood up, Natasha and Troy came up to me with their calendars opened. Troy said, "Chris, I really like the start you've made to the Cheat Sheet. When can the three of us get together? The sooner the better!"

We agreed to each add our thoughts to the Cheat Sheet, share it with a few associates from our teams for input, and then meet on Friday to share results. We would then put a final version together in time for our offsite team meeting.

I walked back to my desk with so many thoughts swimming in my head. As soon as I arrived, I sat down and opened my journal to review what I had written and to organize my thoughts.

- *Cheat Sheet.*

- *Ask HR who trainer is.*

- *Check with associates by Friday.*

- *Ask Stephanie about interview tips.*

- *Weekly Tally.*

I recorded all the new meetings in my calendar, and added time tomorrow to check in with three team associates for their feedback. I underlined asking Stephanie about interview tips and to call HR in the morning to identify who in Training I should speak to about the Cheat Sheet. It wasn't even lunchtime yet!

7

Managing Differences

After reviewing my e-mails, I opened my journal to prepare for my next meeting with Stephanie. It seemed like weeks (instead of one day) since I last met with her. I looked at the questions she asked me to answer before we met again. I started a clean page with today's date, and began jotting down some notes.

- *What have I accomplished since our last meeting?*

  I looked over my list, and realized how much I really had accomplished. The lunch meeting with my fellow supervisory team, the subsequent meeting when I saw the E + R = O in action, and a good start on the Cheat Sheet.

- *What didn't I get done but intended to?*

  I learned a little bit more about reports, but still didn't understand how to pull them from the computer.

- *The challenges and problems I am facing now.*

  This was a long list: interview tips, how to make sure I was getting accountability from staff rather than babysitting them, better balancing work and family life along with time management, how to run a productive team meeting, developing a Weekly Tally.

- *The opportunity that is available to me right now.*

  Hmm…I think it's just survival at this point, and to absorb all I can.

- *I want to use my coach time to…*

  Learn how to get the most from my team meeting, interview tips, balancing time.

I was ready to go visit Stephanie. I grabbed my journal and pen and started toward her office. As I was walking, Natasha joined me. She said timidly, "I know I said I'd work on this Cheat Sheet, but I really don't have any idea what to do, and I've got so many things on my plate already. Do you think you and Troy could take a first stab at it without me?"

I was stunned. "Natasha, I don't think that's fair. We agreed to do it together," I continued, "and you really might learn something in the process."

She lifted her eyebrow in surprise. "Oh, I see," she said. She turned and walked away.

My hands broke out in a sweat. I think I had just blown it with Natasha.

As I approached Stephanie's door, she waved me in. "Hi, Chris." She looked at me closely. "You look like you've just run a marathon. Are you OK?"

I swallowed hard and then relayed what had just happened in the hallway with Natasha. Stephanie thoughtfully stroked her chin and then nodded. "I'm not surprised by either your reaction or Natasha's," she said. "The very natural first response to stress is programmed in us from our prehistoric ancestors is to either flee or fight. However, since we are dependent on each other to work together, neither of those is the best choice today. There are alternative ways to deal with conflict. Do you have any experience with managing differences?"

"Well," I laughed, "I have lots of experience with my family!"

She nodded in agreement. "Yes, that's true. What happens when your daughter is involved in some sort of disagreement?"

I thought for a few seconds and then said, "Well, when she has a disagreement with a close friend, I encourage her to calm down and talk with the friend when she's ready to talk civilly. I remind her to sit down together, listen to her friend, and try to work out their differences. Usually, they figure out a solution that works for both of them."

"It certainly sounds like it works, though, right?" Stephanie replied.

I paused and then replied, "Yes, it does. I believe that we can only control our own actions. Hmm, I guess it's really the same thing with Natasha. I suppose I should go back to Natasha and find out what is really causing her to be so resistant to working on this together and get things back on the right foot."

Defining What You Value

Stephanie nodded, pointing to the framed saying on the wall that I had noticed yesterday, *Do what you value; value what you do.* "When I'm confronted with a sticky situation like this, I use these criteria to help me think it through and decide if I'm acting on my beliefs. She reached into her file drawer, pulled out a piece of paper. Handing it to me, she said, Here's how it works."

I looked at the paper she had given me:

The Seven Criteria for Defining What You Value

It must be prized and cherished.
It must be chosen from among alternatives.
It must be chosen freely, without coercion.
It must be chosen after thoughtful consideration of the consequences of each alternative, not impulsively, and after careful critical thinking.
We must be willing to publicly affirm it.
We must act on it, and act on it repeatedly.
It must be consistent with the other values we profess.

Used with permission from Dr. Sidney B. Simon, Professor Emeritus, Psychological Education, University of Massachusetts

"But," Stephanie emphasized, "before we apply it to the situation with you and Natasha, let me explain each of the criteria using one of my beliefs, which is to balance work and family life."

I sat up to listen intently since, based on last evening, I wasn't doing a very good job balancing my work and family life.

"This belief is very important to me," Stephanie explained, "because I really love the work I do, *and* spending time raising my daughter and being a part of my family is equally important. It's chosen freely, since no one is forcing me to like work or my family. I've thought about what might happen if I didn't balance, and I realize that I wouldn't do a good job with either because I wouldn't be happy just always working, or always being with my family.

"I'm willing to publicly affirm it," she continued. "For example, when I'm asked to work late on a project, I am clear that I have to check my family obligations first before I'll make that commitment. In fact, I've had to do that repeatedly on different projects, because balance is so important to me." She paused and looked at me. "Is this making sense so far?"

I nodded my head yes. This really made sense. I shared with Stephanie what happened last night, almost entirely missing my daughter's soccer tryouts. She empathized, sharing her own challenges of staying true to her decision to balance work and family time.

"We usually get a gut feeling when we're doing something that's not consistent with what we really, really want," Stephanie explained. "Just as you were upset about not keeping your promise to your daughter, I imagine you felt the same way after your interaction with Natasha. It's important to you to do what you say you're going to do, so it's difficult when someone else responds differently. You may have wished you had responded differently, or felt that you just don't like to leave issues unfinished."

I thought about what she said. "I just said exactly what I thought, but I didn't think about how she'd react, and I didn't expect her to walk away, either," I replied. "I'm just realizing that I like to keep the air cleared and have the opportunity to work things out. And, yes, keeping promises is important to me."

I quickly told her about my earlier conversation with Tiko, and how the $E + R = O$ formula had really worked.

Stephanie nodded enthusiastically. "You've caught on quickly. That's also a good example of the remaining values criteria," she continued. "Your belief must be consistent with all other actions. For example, if balance is truly important to me, then when one of my co-workers says they can't work late because of a family obligation, or they ask for vacation time, I respect what's really important to them even if I have to adjust other deadlines."

She paused, then added, "So, when I'm not sure what to do, I test my reaction and my plan against the criteria, which helps me stay on the path I want to be on."

I thought to myself what a really helpful process she was sharing with me. "Now we've started to figure out why the situation with Natasha is uncomfortable for you," Stephanie continued. "It really violated two of your core values—keeping the air clear and sticking to promises, right?"

Stephanie was right on the mark. "That's exactly right," I said and then with a puzzled look, added, "but I'm still a bit confused. What happens when the two of us value different things?"

Self Mediation Technique

Stephanie laughed. "That's the important question, and the answer is we have to use different tools to help manage our differences," she explained.

Surprised, and somewhat confused, I asked, "Is there really a way to manage differences between people with very divergent points of view?"

Stephanie nodded. "Yes." She paused, and then added, "Managing differences doesn't always work 100% of the time. Sometimes we have to agree to disagree, and sometimes we have such different beliefs that we can't reach a solution. The good news, though, is that if both parties are willing to talk, and both want a winning solution, it is possible to manage differences without compromising what's important to each person. Like the example you gave me with your daughter and her friends. They work out their differences because they value their relationship with each other."

"Hmmm, so what can I do with this situation with Natasha?" I asked.

"Well," Stephanie replied, "I've used a process I learned when I took a class with Dr. Dan Dana, author of *Managing Differences*, that I think can be applied to this situation. I've used these steps countless times, both at home and work, and they've really helped get me more win-win situations.

Self Mediation

Find a Time to Talk
Plan the Context
Talk it Out
Make a Deal

Used with permission from Dr. Dan Dana
www.mediationworks.com

"The first step is to approach Natasha at an appropriate time and place, and ask when you can meet to discuss your differences," Stephanie said. "When you approach her, identify what you want to talk about, without blaming or criticizing, and request time to do so. It might sound something like, 'Natasha, do you have a minute to talk about something? I'm uncomfortable about our earlier conversation about how our sub-committee will work together. I'd like to meet with you at your convenience to talk about this so we can reach an agreement. Are you willing?'"

I thought about it and said, "It sounds good, but I think she'll just say no, she doesn't have the time, like she did before."

"You might be right to expect resistance or rejection," Stephanie replied. "You then have to 'sell' your proposal to meet, just like you sell our products on the phone with customers. First, acknowledge her objections, then show how acceptance would benefit her interest, and repeat your request."

I was now writing furiously in my journal. I looked back up to Stephanie and said, "I'm stuck on what the benefit to Natasha would be."

"OK," said Stephanie, "then let's think about benefits to Natasha. She'd really benefit because, as you go through the Cheat Sheet, she'd be learning the process and be one step ahead of everyone else. Even if she doesn't have improvement ideas for the worksheet, she'd have a role in how it's introduced to the team. This would likely make her feel more comfortable with the communication and coaching."

"I understand now," I said. "I think we really need her, too, because she was on the product development team and really understands product."

Stephanie nodded in agreement. "Those are reasons for her to be part of the team. How will this help her with her time crunch, which seems to be her biggest concern?" she asked.

"Hmm...well," I thought about it. "She won't have to train on it because she'll already know it," I said.

"Good point," Stephanie encouraged. "So put it all together, and remember to repeat your request."

I made a few quick notes and then took a deep breath. "OK, here goes."

I practiced out loud: "Natasha, do you have a minute to talk about something? I'm uncomfortable about our earlier conversation in the hallway. I understand you don't think you'll have time to work on the Cheat Sheet sub-committee. I'd like to meet with you at your convenience to talk about this so we can reach an agreement on how we'll work together. Are you willing?"

"Good," Stephanie said confidently. "Now what do you say when Natasha says she really doesn't have time to talk about it, let alone do the work!"

I took another deep breath. "I'd say: 'I understand how busy you are. My hunch is that working with us will end up saving you time because you won't have to go to training, nor will the Cheat Sheet have to be redone time and time again, because you'll have shared all the product knowledge from your experience on the development team. I want to avoid any of us wasting additional time. How about meeting to see how it'll work out best for all of us?'"

Stephanie clapped. "You sound like a pro mediator, Chris! Being optimistic, let's say Natasha agrees to meet with you. Ask her to choose the time and place, as long as you are comfortable with the suggestion. This usually should be in a fairly private area. Then summarize what you've both agreed to—'So, we'll meet in the conference room on the third floor from 3:30 to 4 this afternoon, right?'"

"Wow, this is beginning to sound complicated," I said.

Stephanie nodded empathetically. "There are many things to think about at first, but once you do it a few times, it'll seem very natural. Are you ready to absorb the rest of it?" she asked.

"I think so. If not, I'll come back to ask you more questions!" I said.

"You can always stop by to clarify something, or even leave me a voicemail," Stephanie said. "There are also a few others in the company who have been trained by Dr. Dana. Your boss, Peter, and David were both in the class with me."

"Oh, that's good, in case I have a question when you're not around!" I said.

"Let's continue so you have the whole process," Stephanie said. She went on to explain that before the meeting begins, there are two "cardinal rules", as Dr. Dana calls them. "First, you agree not to permit any interruptions or to walk out or stop trying until the agreed-upon time has expired. Secondly, agree not to use any type of power or force to override the other's objections, or develop a one-sided solution," she explained.

"Once you have agreement on the cardinal rules, you're ready to begin talking it out," Stephanie continued. "This next part is what has been most helpful to me.

"Dr. Dana recommends beginning the meeting with an opening that expresses appreciation and optimism. Something like, 'I appreciate your willingness to meet with me to talk this out. I'm hopeful that we can find a solution beneficial to both of us.' These statements will get things off to a positive start. Then, agree on the cardinal rules, and state the issue again, with an invitation to first ask how she sees the situation," she said.

"For example," Stephanie said, "Natasha, my understanding is that you're really crunched for time, and I really want you to make time to help put the Cheat Sheet together. Please tell me how you see the situation and how this affects you.'"

I wrote what Stephanie said. It sounded so polished, but I didn't think I could get the words out so optimistically.

Stephanie must have read my thoughts. "Chris, I know it may sound difficult. I stumbled a little bit at first, but it really does work," she said. "Once the dialogue begins, you can usually reach a breakthrough by understanding her position, and having her understand yours. Then, suddenly, an alternative pops up that solves the issue for both of you!"

"Well, I'm willing to give it a try," I said. "It couldn't make it any worse, that's for sure!"

"Wonderful," said Stephanie. "I look forward to hearing how it goes. And don't worry if it's not perfect the first time, or if Natasha doesn't want to try to work it out. At least you've tried!"

"You're right Stephanie," I said. "I'll have to try it out at home, too!"

Interview Tips

I looked at my watch. We had another 15 minutes together. "Stephanie, we don't have time to get to everything I wanted to talk to you about today. However, I have two critical topics I need your advice on before we end our session. First, I'm having my first team meeting tomorrow, and second, I'm meeting with Tiko to set up our process for interviewing for our open positions. I've really done neither, so I wondered what wisdom you might share with me in the time we have left."

Stephanie grinned. "We could spend a month on each, and still not have enough time," she said. "Quickly, though, I can offer a few tips. Think about what you want to accomplish in your first team meeting. One of the most important things is to 'set a climate' of mutual respect, and target the reachable goals, always remembering the Values criteria. There are always alternatives, or more than one way to accomplish the same goal, so stay open to new ideas."

"Perfect!" I exclaimed. "That's just what I needed to get my thoughts organized—Set the Climate, Target Goals and Review Alternatives—I've got it. Now, how about interviews?"

"You really make the most of every minute, don't you?" Stephanie laughed. "OK, 5 minutes of wisdom about interviews. The most important thing to remember is that past performance predicts future performance. Ask the candidate to *describe* how they've accomplished a goal or met a customer's need, or how they've handled a sticky situation. Make sure they tell you stories about the past, rather than what they *would* do. Feed off their answers and dive into deeper detail about the situation so that you're sure they're consistent and not making up the story." She paused and waited for me to make notes in my journal.

I looked back up and said, "I hear that interview questions are really important. How do you know if the candidates will fit into this kind of work, and if they really have the 'gene' for servicing customers?"

She was silent for a minute. "That's a good question and it comes with some experience. Listen for the words they use to talk about themselves and others, and trust your gut," she shared. "Make sure you have them observe the job being done, and talk about the difficult parts as well as the benefits of the job. Finally, listen to what questions they ask. If they come with none, they really haven't thought much about the job. Or if they ask questions only about salary or work hours, you may need to dig deeper into their real motives for seeking a job change."

"These are really helpful, Stephanie," I said. "I think I should bring a tape recorder next time. I can hardly write everything down! Thank you for the wonderful ideas. I'll do my best to remember them all."

"You're welcome. Give yourself a little bit of slack," she added. "You'll make mistakes, but you'll learn from them, too. Feel free to bring a tape recorder if it'll make it easier for you."

"Let's see," she said looking at her calendar, frowning, "We're scheduled to meet for the next three days, but I've been unexpectedly pulled into a senior management meeting, and I'm getting ready for your offsite team meeting. I'm going to have to push us off until next week. Will next Tuesday at 10 a.m. work for you?"

"We've covered a lot of ground today, and I have plenty of things to do," I said. "Sure, Tuesday at 10 is fine. I'm sure I'll have a ton to talk about!"

"Chris, remember you have other teammates who have done these things before too," Stephanie added. "You can lean on them if you really get stuck."

"You're right, Stephanie," I said. "I do need to get over this thing of trying to be perfect in front of others. See you next week."

Practicing Conflict Resolution

I walked back to my desk thinking about how to approach Natasha, when she came around the corner. Well, I thought, nothing like the present to tackle this one! She started to avoid eye contact with me. As she almost walked by me, I turned and said, "Natasha, do you have a few minutes to talk about something?"

Natasha slowly turned my way, but didn't attempt to make eye contact, and flatly replied, "Well...I'm kind of wrapped up right now, what can I do for you?" I swallowed nervously, and tried to remember what I had just practiced with Stephanie. I wasn't sure I had everything committed to memory, but I continued anyway. "I wondered if you would be willing to meet with me at your convenience for a few minutes so we can agree on how to proceed with this Cheat Sheet as I *really* value your input," I said.

Natasha looked irritated and then said with frustration, "Um, it's just that I'm *so* busy...but," she perked up, "I was just heading to the cafeteria for an early lunch. I could come over to your desk and eat while we talk—I have about 30 minutes before I need to get back to my desk. Like I said earlier, I don't have time for everything I need to get done."

"That'd be great. I'll see you in a few minutes, then?" Natasha nodded, and stepped away. It wasn't perfect, but at least it worked to get me to the next step. It sure felt different for me to approach it this way.

I looked at the notes I had taken in my journal, and had just started moving folders off the other chair when Natasha arrived. I smiled and said, "I really appreciate your willingness to help with this, and I don't think it will take the whole 30 minutes to come up with a solution that will work for everyone. I hit the button on my phone to send my calls into voicemail. Is that OK with you?" I held my breath and hoped I didn't get bombarded with her time management issues, since we had a task to complete.

Natasha nodded as she looked down at her lunch. She said humbly, "Chris, it's not like I don't want to do the work. I'm just trying to use my time wisely. And you guys are so much better at this customer stuff that I just figured that it's better if I wait until you have a draft."

Pointing to the mess I had just cleared, I said, "I understand your point that you're crunched for time. But, my hunch is that we will all end up saving time if we do it together. You've got more product knowledge than Troy or me and I really want you to be part of putting the final draft together. Since you and I are meeting first, maybe I can share your thoughts with Troy to get it pulled together more quickly. What do you think?"

Natasha paused in thought. "Chris, I do want to be a team player and help create the process. So, if it's product knowledge that you need, why don't I take a stab at drafting those parts of the form first? I prefer having time to think about things and get them down on paper. That way, when we meet, we won't waste time coming up with all of the products that should be on the Cheat Sheet, and our time will be much more productive."

"I see your point," I said. "The other parts would flow more quickly if we had an outline of the products to start with." But a part of me was concerned that if I turned it over, she wouldn't have the time to do it.

Natasha continued, with some excitement in her voice, "I can also go back to my notes from the marketing meetings and look up the comments we received when we interviewed customers. There were all kinds of benefits they told us about that we could capture on the Cheat Sheet. If I could use the original time we set aside on Friday, I could work on it then, and a little bit after the kids go to sleep," she winked, "and I have some time while I watch my son's soccer game this weekend. I could e-mail you what I come up with on Monday morning, and maybe squeeze in an hour over lunch."

Thinking about my own weekend schedule, I asked, "What soccer team does your son play on? My daughter just tried out for a travel team."

"He's on the city recreational travel team," Natasha answered. "It's the first time he'll be playing on the home field, and I promised I'd get there this weekend. Do you think your daughter will make the team?"

"Issues are like stones. If you pick them up one by one, they're easy to move. If you pile them up, they become a weight that drags you down."

www.callcentercoach.com
Call Center INSIDER Newsletter

Balancing Time

"I hope so," I chuckled, "although I'll be in the same boat as yours trying to squeeze in one more thing!" Turning back, I pulled out my calendar. "Given all of the other things piling up, I think we should plot out a quick plan so we'll be ready for the team meeting."

Looking over what we had jotted down, it certainly made sense to me. "Let's see if we can reach Troy to make sure the new plan works for him," I said. I turned back to my phone, found Troy's extension number and left a voicemail for him suggesting the changes, asking him to contact me about his availability. Turning back to Natasha, I said, "I'll pencil in Monday lunch for us to get together. In the meantime, I'll see if I can use Friday to meet with the trainer from Human Resources and maybe Troy could check in with Shawn from Scheduling. We'll need input from a few associates, too."

Smiling, I said, "I think it would be easier if Troy saw this new plan in an e-mail, and I can make those suggestions. I think this is actually a better solution." And I could see from Natasha's expression that it was a much better plan for her too.

We looked at our calendars and scheduled some short meetings to check in with each other. I e-mailed the schedule to Troy, along with the suggestion to meet with Shawn. "If Troy can't make these times," Natasha said looking at her notes, "I could change a few things around on Tuesday so we can get a final draft ready for our meeting."

"OK, I'll keep that in mind," I said. I looked at my watch, and said, "We're one minute over what we said we'd spend on this, but we probably spent that minute talking about soccer. Anyway, thanks for taking the time out to work this through."

Natasha grinned. "No problem...I just feel so overwhelmed most of the time," she said. "This job is a whole lot more difficult than meets the eye."

Natasha stood up and gathered her things. Lightly, she said, "Well, hopefully this Cheat Sheet will help all of us save time and help us better manage our results."

I nodded in agreement. "I sure hope so," I said. "We'll just have to make sure Troy agrees." We said our good-byes and agreed to communicate over email as needed.

Well, well, well. The process for managing differences actually worked! I could hardly wait to tell Stephanie.

8

Working As a Team

I opened my day planner and looked at the list of things remaining to be done today. Getting my first team meeting off the ground was on the "A" priority list. Scheduling had sent me an e-mail letting me know I could have time tomorrow afternoon for a meeting, so I wanted to get the invitation and agenda distributed today. I picked up the journal Stephanie had given me and turned to the comments I had written from my coaching session. I then opened up a new document on my computer. I thought back to how Holly, my former supervisor, had run her meetings. I really liked the fact that there was always a mixture of business and learning at each of them.

Setting Expectations

First I typed in my desired outcomes for the meeting. I remembered the clarity of Peter's agenda and the meeting objectives so everyone knew what to expect. And I really liked his ground rules, which seemed to keep things on track. This would be important for me, since one of my personal limitations was managing time effectively during meetings. I also saw the value of posting action items, as well as ending the meeting with a Plus/Delta process as a way to review results, changes and actions.

What I Want to Accomplish at My First Team Meeting:

Set a Climate of Mutual Respect
Get to Know Each Person
Set Ground Rules
Establish Target Goals
Review Sales Goals
Set Up Expectations for One-on-One Coaching
Learn One New Thing
Open Microphone
Plus/Delta

I decided to use these goals to prepare an agenda. It would probably be hard to squeeze in all of these things, so I'd have to postpone a few until the next meeting. I worked and reworked the agenda, trying diligently to plan the amount of time needed to cover each topic. After an hour, I had assembled an e-mail invitation with an agenda and finally was ready to hit the "Send" button. I read it one more time to be sure the tone was positive, expectations were clear, and I had the appropriate amount of time allotted for each topic:

Dear Team Members,

I am delighted to be serving you as your new supervisor. Scheduling has arranged for phone coverage so we can have our first team meeting from 2:30-3:45 p.m. tomorrow in the Team Conference room. Please plan to attend!

My goals are that we get to know one another a bit more, review how we're doing on our sales and service targets and brainstorm ways we can improve them. Please review the following agenda and come prepared to participate! I hope this is the start of us being a top performing team for our company.

Sincerely,

Chris Crandall

Team Meeting Agenda
2:30-3:45 p.m. Thursday/Team Conference Room

Ice Breaker: Who Am I?	10 minutes
Team Ground Rules	20 minutes
Sales and Service Goals	15 minutes
Review Development Process	5 minutes
Learn to Earn Skill	10 minutes
Open Microphone	10 minutes
Review Action Items/Plus/Delta	5 minutes

Everything appeared to be in order, so the invitation went out. Boy did it feel good to complete a task on my to-do list!

I returned to my e-mails and found a reply from Tina, a member of the corporate training team. I had sent a note to her describing the Cheat Sheet project and requesting a referral to the appropriate Training resource. Her e-mail directed me to meet with Larry Smith, although I'd have to work around his training schedule. That meant before 8 a.m. or after 5 p.m. Maybe I could bring Lanie to school early tomorrow or the next morning and fit in a meeting with Larry. I sent a note to Larry to see if he could prepare materials with such short notice and asked when the best time was to meet with him.

There was another e-mail from Troy letting me know the scheduled meeting times—for the preparation work and to complete the Cheat Sheet Natasha and I had sent him—worked fine. It seemed like I was becoming a manager of schedules, keeping track of all of these follow-up meetings. I hoped I was remembering everything. My thoughts were interrupted by the phone ringing.

"Good-afternoon, this is Chris. How may I help you?"

Ethics and Integrity Take a Stand

"Hi Chris, this is Peter. I need to pull you into an emergency meeting about one of your employees. Could you come down to my office?"

His voice sounded serious. I felt my stomach drop. What could be prompting an emergency meeting? It didn't sound like good news. I gulped, and then said, "Sure, Peter, I'll be right down."

My heart was racing by the time I reached Peter's office. Sitting at his desk was Hank, the head of Human Resources. Both of them looked solemn.

As I walked in the door, Peter said, "Chris thanks for interrupting your day and coming down. Have a seat." He pointed to an empty chair next to Hank. "Now that both of you are here, let me review what has been brought to my attention."

Peter continued. "Yesterday I asked Navya, our Quality Control Analyst, to provide me with last quarter's quality trend report. I was reviewing it to help me prepare for our offsite meeting next week. I noticed that Charlie is one of our top salespeople this quarter, and in fact, is in line for a healthy bonus. I decided it would be a good idea to listen to some of his calls to identify the reasons for his success, so perhaps we could all share in some best practices. I'd like to play for you what I heard."

Peter turned to his computer and clicked on the audio playback system. Charlie's voice came in loud and clear. The customer was looking for an inventory solution, and it was apparent that our Inventory Scanner was a good solution. I listened to Charlie explain to the customer the benefits of tracking his inventory more accurately and how it would save him time. Then I heard Charlie tell the customer that he was obligated to purchase the Power Shelf product to take advantage of our special pricing for the Inventory Scanner. "What?" I muttered in an exasperated tone. This was not true! These were both stand-alone products!

The call resulted in the customer reluctantly buying both products, and Charlie lining his pocket with a healthy commission, since the Power Shelf was clearly the more profitable product. Peter clicked the audio to stop playing and said, "We've given Charlie a warning about stretching the marketing rules in the past, but this is clearly a misrepresentation of our products and services, which is a serious offense and grounds for dismissal. Chris, I know this is not a pleasant job for a supervisor, but it has to be done. You'll need to let Charlie know that he is terminated based on the fact that he has violated our code of conduct and ethics. Hank has already drafted a message to our staff restating our company policy on integrity and honesty. The word will get around quickly, so I want to be sure we take a strong stance on this issue. There may be several people who will feel Charlie was treated unfairly. You'll need to be ready to respond to them."

"OK," I said slowly, still in shock. I remembered that Charlie's son was being treated for cancer. Several peers had conducted fund-raisers over the last few months to help him cover expenses. Hank interrupted my thoughts and let me know that he'd be ready as soon as we reviewed the procedures and collaborated on what I would say to Charlie. We also went over a few questions Hank thought I might get from my team members.

After about 20 minutes of discussion, Hank and I walked to his office. My hands were shaking. Hank then dialed Charlie's extension and asked him to come down to the Human Resources office.

As Charlie walked in the door, he looked distraught. Hank asked him to sit down, turned to me and nodded his head for me to begin. "Charlie, this is a difficult meeting to have with you," I said, "Navya has documented more than 15 calls this quarter where you charged customers for things they did not order or misrepresented price quotes." I paused and took a deep breath. "And we *cannot* reward this type of behavior, no matter what the circumstances; therefore we're going to have to terminate your employment with us." I had such mixed emotions as I looked at Charlie as he absorbed the news.

Charlie was red as a beet, and then said defensively, "I was just trying to make some extra income for my son's medical expenses. I know it wasn't right, but I couldn't help myself. You'd probably do the same thing if you were in my shoes. I'm sorry. Can't you give me another chance?"

I didn't know what to say. Thankfully, Hank stepped in and said, "Charlie, you've already received a warning about this. Navya has documented the calls during which you inappropriately sold products, and your commission for this quarter will be adjusted accordingly. We will mail you your final paycheck next week. I'll accompany you to your desk to get your things."

Charlie had nothing else to say. I stood up as Hank walked Charlie out to his desk. I was stunned. How could Charlie do such a thing? He was our best salesperson, people looked up to him, and lately everyone had been especially supportive because of his family situation. I slowly walked back to my desk.

I was staring at my computer when Hank walked up. I invited him to sit down. "Chris, I wish that none of us ever had to deal with this sort of issue. It's painful and no one really wins. I think the most critical response is honesty without judgment," he continued. "Our policy on confidentially prevents you from discussing any details, but it is clear that this was a decision based on our company's stance on ethics and integrity. You'll need to remind your team of those policies and that breaking those policies are grounds for immediate dismissal.

"Peter mentioned that you have a team meeting this afternoon. That would be a good time to remind your team of our policies," he said. "I think others will be empathetic, yet understand that we act on our company and personal values. If you are unsure of how to handle specific questions, you can give me a call."

I remembered the conversation with Stephanie about "Do what you value; value what you do," and how important it was to act on our values repeatedly and consistently. I wondered if Charlie had ever thought about the possible consequences of his actions, or alternatives. He was a talented person and could have earned his commission honestly.

Hank interrupted my thoughts. "Chris, I trust that you'll say the right thing when asked and that you'll handle this situation professionally," he said. "If you get stuck, and I'm not available, David has experience with handling difficult questions. He had to handle a similar situation some years ago, so if you need a peer to run your thoughts by, he'd be another good choice."

"Hank, thanks for your vote of confidence," I replied. "I'll do the best I can."

"I know you will treat the situation sensitively," Hank said as he left my office.

My shock slowly began to turn to anger. I had this sinking feeling that if anyone knew about what Charlie had been doing, they might try the same tactics, or worse yet, look away and say nothing! It was not going to be easy to handle such issues with sensitivity and honesty, but I knew that ultimately each employee needed to be responsible for his or her own actions.

As I thought about what Hank said, Peter dropped in and asked how it went. "This is never easy, Chris," he said. "I'm concerned that some of Charlie's peers may have overheard what he was doing and saw how it was impacting his commission. I want you to work with Navya and review the higher revenue producers, and listen to their calls to see if we have anyone else we need to deal with." I nodded solemnly.

"And," Peter added, "I want you to review each of the customer profiles of the remaining calls that Navya has, and determine if we need to take any corrective action. I'm concerned about our reputation. The last thing we need is for customers to find out we've mistreated them, and spread a negative message about us to the marketplace. I've already called and refunded money to the customer who was charged for the product he didn't really want or need," he continued. "I will be advising the whole supervisory staff at our next meeting in case anyone gets a complaint. Finally, I'll let you know if we'll be replacing Charlie. I know you already have one vacancy on your team. I'm not sure I want you to take on two brand new hires this soon. And since his results have inflated our overall results, I need to take a serious look at the possibility of reaching our goals the honest way."

I hadn't even thought about filling Charlie's shoes. "Tiko and I are interviewing candidates over the next few days. I could keep this in mind, and let you know if we have three winners."

Peter paused for a moment. "That makes sense," he said, "especially if we can get them all into the same new hire class that begins in a few weeks. But don't just hire for the sake of filling a vacancy. It's better to be short-handed than to have a poorly matched employee for the job. I'll let you know more after I've talked with Scheduling about shift needs and team size."

We discussed when I'd give Peter a status report on my findings and the actions I was empowered to take with customers to build their confidence in our company. As I walked back to my office, I looked over to where Charlie's station used to be. It was completely empty. It seemed such a shame that this had to happen.

David flagged me down just as I turned the corner to my office. "Chris, do you have a minute?" he asked.

"Sure," I said, looking around. I felt like all eyes were on me. David sat down, and said, "I just saw Charlie escorted out. What's up?"

I let out a long sigh and told David what had happened. He whistled under his breath. "Wow, this will be a blow to our whole office. I had a similar issue a few years back," he shared. "I wish I could tell you it's going to be easy, but I think you need to be ready to ride it out."

David told me quickly about what had happened with one of his employees. "The most important lesson I learned was it's best not to share any specific details, yet make yourself available to your team," he said. "The quicker everyone gets it out of their systems, the faster things return to normal."

"That's exactly what Peter and Hank said," I shared. "Hank from Human Resources is already sending out our ethics and conduct policy. "I'll let you get back to work," David replied, "but if you need anyone to lean on or commiserate with, give me a call. I know I was ready to have a long break after it was all over."

"Thanks, I'll let you know if I need some backup support." I said, forcing a smile.

By the time I turned to my computer and started reading through my e-mail, Hank had already sent the memo to all associates reminding them of our policies.

There was also a message from Larry from training. He was confirming that tomorrow morning at 7:30 would work for him, and told me which room to meet him in. I made a copy of the Cheat Sheet and put it on my desk so I could grab it before the meeting.

I was ready to call it a day. It certainly had unexpected turns, but I was glad that I had accomplished a few things. I was leaving a little bit late again, but this time I would to be home in time to take Lanie shopping for soccer cleats, as I'd promised.

Getting Grounded Again

After shoe shopping, we went home, had a quick dinner and did some chores. I looked through the mail and e-mail, checked Lanie's homework, and finally walked upstairs to sleep. I was exhausted and fell asleep dreaming about facilitating my first team meeting.

The next day, I dropped Lanie off at school early and made my way to the training room to meet Larry. "Good morning, Larry. I'm Chris, the new team supervisor. Thanks for agreeing to get here a little earlier today to meet with me," I said.

"It's nice to meet you, Chris. I've heard you're doing a special project to help agents learn to sell our new products," Larry said. "I'm excited to hear you're working on it, since you've just come from the front line and can help us all with making training realistic. How can I help you?" he asked.

I pulled the draft Cheat Sheet out and showed it to Larry, explaining how I thought it would work to have a summary sheet of common customer needs, questions to ask customers, how customers talk about the pain points, and then how to position our products and services.

"This looks awesome!" Larry exclaimed.

"Thanks," I replied. "What our project team needs is a complete list of all our new products and services that will be coming out, along with their features and benefits."

"I have several summary sheets of the new products and services and their features," Larry responded. "I'll check with Marketing, too. They conducted focus groups in which customers talked about their concerns, as well as features they would like our products and services to provide for their businesses. Marketing uses that information to determine the specifications of our new products and services. They usually give us a summary of those conversations so we can use them as case studies in training. When do you need them by?"

"Larry, both resources would be super!" I said. "We're meeting the first of next week to finalize the draft, and will then share it with our entire supervisory staff during our quarterly meeting. Is it possible to have the information that soon?"

"It's a little tight, but I'll make a few calls during break today," he replied. "I'll let you know if I'll have a problem getting it to you by the end of the week. Otherwise expect an e-mail with attachments from me within the next day or so."

"Thank you for the extra effort," I said. "I'll certainly make sure you get a copy of what we come up with. Hopefully it will support you in training as well."

Larry smiled. "In fact, I'll ask you for a return favor when the new hire class begins," he said. "I'm always looking for guest speakers to introduce the sales and service process and demonstrate examples of working with our customers."

I grinned enthusiastically. "I'd actually enjoy doing that," I said. "I used to have new hires come work with me at my desk during their training, and I always found it refreshing and rewarding when I could help someone new to understand our customers."

"Wonderful, then," Larry concluded. "I'll be in touch when the time comes."

I left the room feeling exuberant. The Cheat Sheet was going to be better than ever. As I walked back to my office, I started dreaming about the possibility of putting it online. "Whoa, Chris, don't get ahead of yourself," I thought. But I still jotted down the idea in my journal when I returned to my office.

The morning flew by as I read reports David had sent out regarding our results. I could see what he meant by the amount of data and how it really needed to be summarized so we could see how we're doing at a quick glance. As I flipped to the last page, Tim from my team came to my door and asked if I had a few minutes to speak with him. He looked a bit tentative, so I immediately invited him in and asked him to take a seat.

"What's on your mind?" I asked, trying to make him feel at ease.

"It's about Charlie," he said, his voice shaking. "I just came in for my shift and heard he was escorted out. Then I saw the memo from Human Resources. I sit right next to where he sat, and I overheard several of the calls during which he didn't do things exactly right. My sales are at the bottom of the whole team, because I wouldn't misrepresent information to our clients just to make a sale. I won't get any commission this quarter, and in fact, I'm on warning from my previous supervisor. If I don't get my sales up, I'm going to lose my job."

He was shaking so much by this time that he had to take a deep breath to continue. "I really can't afford not to work," he said. "I was wondering if you could help me figure out how to improve, since I really don't understand what to do differently?"

I sighed with relief. At least Tim wasn't going to give me a hard time about Charlie's dismissal. I had an idea. "Tim, first, I'm really glad that you came to talk with me, and I especially admire that you have been honest with our customers and with me. One of my job responsibilities is to be sure all of my team members are successful, so I will absolutely do whatever I can to help you. In fact, I've been working on a Cheat Sheet to share with the whole staff to help improve their sales. I need some different associates to test it out before we release it across the floor. Would you like to be among the first to try it out?"

Tim's eyes lit up, and he enthusiastically said, "Absolutely! When can I start?"

"Well, it's not done yet," I replied, "but I don't see why you couldn't take what I've got and try it immediately. I don't have all of the new products and services on it yet, but you could use it and let me know if the format is easy to use and if the information works for you."

"Chris, I seem to be really successful at resolving customer's issues. I know I resolve about 80% of customer issues; the other 20% are not within my authority, so I've escalated them. I'm seeing that for those 80%, I make offers on just about half of them, so I'm trying to see how I can figure out an offer to make on all of them. Will this Cheat Sheet help me?"

"Yes, Tim. I think it will certainly get you started in the right direction," I said. "The other part of the equation is tuning into what the customer is saying and sometimes what they're *not* saying. Let's start with the Cheat Sheet, and then I can listen and coach you on specific calls."

After we reviewed it and I explained how I thought it could be used, Tim agreed to give it a try. He would take notes on what he did and didn't use and anything else he tried, along with the outcomes. We agreed to meet first thing on Monday so he could share his notes and thoughts with me. This was perfect timing before my meeting with Natasha and Troy, so we'd have some live input to confirm whether we were heading in the right direction.

By the time the afternoon came, I found myself a bit anxious about my team meeting. The night before I dreamt that I spoke a different language than they did, so we couldn't understand each other. I hoped that wasn't a bad omen!

Team Development Cycle

As everyone gathered in the Team Conference Room the next day, I sensed apprehension in the air. I understood this all too well. I looked at the faces around the table and took a deep breath.

"Good afternoon and thank you for getting here promptly. I think we're all a bit nervous, or at least I am, since this is our first meeting. I am very excited to be your new team supervisor and hope to help us become the best team in the company! Let's review the agenda and then start with our icebreaker."

Everyone shifted in their seats after I reviewed the agenda, seemingly more relaxed. I then introduced the icebreaker. "It's important to me that I get to know each of you, and I will do that during our scheduled one-on-one time," I said. "I also want us, as a team, to know what strengths we each bring to the team to make us successful as a group. I'd like you to think a few minutes about your strengths and share them with the group by using words that either start with or include your first and last name initials. For example, I'm Chris Crandall, so the descriptions I use will have two C's in them. I'll start. One of my strengths is that I'm *customer-focused*, and the other is that I like to *coach* others to be successful. The letters don't necessarily have to be at the beginning of the word. Take a few seconds to think about it, and we'll start with the person who has the smallest shoe size."

They all chuckled, and pointed to Miranda Wong, who wore a size 5 shoe. Miranda started by saying, "I love to multi-task and I am a workaholic for customers, since I used to own a small business and have a good understanding of what customers need."

"Solid start, Miranda. And it's good to know we have someone on the team with small business experience. Who's next?" I asked.

Each person selected traits to describe a skill or approach that helped the team. I was truly amazed at what a rich collection of knowledge and positive attitude was sitting in front of me.

"Thank you for sharing your wealth of information," I said. "I learned new things about each of you, and I hope you did too! I'd like to introduce a concept that I first learned when I attended a conference and heard Bruce Tuckman speak. He taught us about the importance of individual team members and their contributions to team success. I learned that individuals really *do* help the team perform like a well-oiled machine."

"The more we all understand what to expect in team development, the better-equipped we'll be to handle difficulties and improve our quality, resulting in 'knock your socks off' performance!" I explained. "Today, I'd like us to learn about the Tuckman's stages of team development, and begin thinking about ground rules that we can agree on that will help us become a high-performing team."

I drew a circle on the flipchart, and divided it into four quadrants.

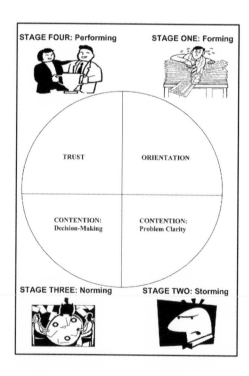

Writing "Stage 1: Forming" in the upper right quadrant, I explained, "Forming is when we're just getting to know one another. We're polite, a little guarded in our conversations, and don't take a lot of risks with each other." I wrote these characteristics in the area of the flipchart titled 'Forming'.

Continuing clockwise to the bottom right quadrant, I said, "The second stage, 'Storming', occurs when we all get clarity about handling problems. It's when we are a bit more comfortable confronting one another, although it may look a bit chaotic at first, or even be uncomfortable for some of us. I've been on some teams where it felt like we were stuck and just arguing with each other endlessly."

"The third stage, 'Norming', occurs when we start understanding each other's personalities, needs and pet peeves and begin looking for common ground. Sometimes teams can become hesitant in making decisions during this stage, but they're learning to deal with differences," I explained.

"The fourth stage, 'Performing', occurs when we reach our true competence as a team. We know how to support one another, are committed to common goals, and learn how to quickly mend our differences. Depending on the issues being raised, changing expectations from our customers or shareholders, or changes in members of the team, teams can move back and forth between these stages."

Establishing Ground Rules

I took a deep breath and stopped. "Does anyone have any questions so far?" I asked.

Tommy piped up. "Chris, no offense, but we're behind in our numbers and I don't see how this is going to help us improve our results."

I was glad Tommy had raised this point. I knew that if one person said something, it was on more than a few minds. "Tommy, you're right from the perspective that this doesn't have an immediate impact on our numbers," I responded. "But learning to work well with each other has a longer-term impact. We'll perform better and be able to sustain our performance. It's like the well-oiled machine I referred to earlier. If a machine isn't maintained with oil frequently, it loses the ability to perform at its best and eventually breaks down. The 'oil' in this case is our ground rules. Does that make sense?"

Tommy nodded his head in agreement and said, "Then, let's get on with it!"

"OK. I have a few ground rules that have worked well for me in the past. I'll jot them down and see if you agree," I said. "These will give us a start, and then we will have about 10 minutes to come up with our team's first set of ground rules. As we work together, we may add or change them." I wrote:

- *Listen carefully to understand intent.*

- *Clarify what you don't understand.*

- *There are no dumb questions.*

"These three are important to me," I said. "In fact, I'll ask everyone to help each other really listen to what another person is saying, to understand their intent. We all filter information differently, depending on the day, person, voice tone, and message or comfort with a topic. It's especially difficult to understand when our perspective or experience is different from what is being said. Once we're committed to listening, then asking for clarification will save us from misunderstandings. Can we all agree?"

Everyone nodded their heads. "What others can you think of that would make you comfortable working together?" I asked.

Tommy piped up: "I think we should say what we mean."

"Let me clarify, Tommy. Do you mean that we need to be honest with each other?" I asked.

"Yes," he said, "and not be afraid to state our opinions. I'd rather know where a person stands than have them beat around the bush."

I added to the flipchart: *Honesty—don't beat around the bush, say what you mean.*

"Tommy, does this capture what you meant?" I asked.

"Yes," he replied.

"OK, team—can we all live with this ground rule?" I asked.

Not everyone nodded. Tonya and Tony appeared uncomfortable. "I see that not all heads are nodding. What's not comfortable about this?" I was hoping Tonya or Tony would speak up, but neither offered any comment. I wasn't sure what to do, since I thought it was an important ground rule.

After a few moments of uncomfortable silence, Tonya quietly said, "It's not that I don't agree with it; I just don't want to agree that people can say whatever they please." She paused, and then continued, "Some of us have a tendency to say things that are personal and not team issues. I'd be OK if we kept our comments to just about the team."

A few people shifted uncomfortably in their seats. I could feel the tension mounting, so I had to do or say something. "I think that over time we'll know what is appropriate during team meetings, and what should be taken outside of the team," I said. "The challenge is that sometimes what's going on personally affects the team, so it's hard to differentiate where it belongs. It is a difficult, but important balance between understanding someone's personal issues and effectively running a business."

Miranda spoke up and said, "How about an additional ground rule that says something like *'respect individuals'* or *'keep discussions to issues, not people'*?"

Everyone around the table nodded. Tonya said, "If we add both of those, I could live with Tommy's suggestion."

I wrote Miranda's suggestions on the flipchart, and paused. "I just want to take a minute and commend everyone for successfully making it around the team development cycle," I said. "We've just had a mini-experience of going through all of the stages. Congratulations!"

The light bulbs going off in their heads was apparent on all of their faces.

"We have time for one more ground rule today," I said, "and then I'd like us all to continue thinking about them. We can add or edit these as we work together."

Raj spoke up: "I'd like to add that we should follow through. In other words, *'say what we'll do, and then do what we say'*. That way, we're all clear about expectations of one another. We know we can't let each other down, or off the hook."

Everyone was nodding enthusiastically, so I added the idea to the flipchart.

"Thanks for all of your contributions. This is an important start to our ground rules," I said. I wrote, *"Type the ground rules and distribute them to the group"* on a flipchart titled, *"Actions"*, and then added my name next to it.

Turning back to the group, I explained, "During our meetings, I'll keep track of our agreements and actions, as well as any specific dates and owners. After the meeting, I'll type up the action items and get them out to you via e-mail so you all have a summary of what we've agreed to do."

I then moved to the next agenda item, reviewing the sales and service goals. They showed how our team was ranked across the company. We were smack in the middle of the pack. I encouragingly said, "I know we can improve on these results and be among the top-ranked teams in the company. I'd like you to turn to the person next to you and, as partners, discuss your ideas and then agree on one thing we could do differently to change our ranking. Let's take about 5 minutes for discussion and be ready to share your best idea. Are there any questions before we begin?"

Gabriella spoke up. "I'm not convinced that we can do anything better, Chris," she said. "Speaking for myself, I've been trying to improve sales results, but customers don't want to buy when they're calling in to complain. I feel lucky if I can solve their problem without them hanging up on me! Maybe I'm the only one, but I'd like to know what the others think."

"I agree," said Kate. "We've been improving steadily, but I think we've already reached our maximum output. I take about 80 calls a day, and the majority of them are returns, complaints, or people who are just shopping around."

These were not the comments I had expected. "How many of you feel this way—that we can't improve our results or ranking?" I asked for a show of hands. The group was split. About 60% thought it was not possible.

"It's important for me to understand your perspective," I said. "Your points are valid and if you don't think it can be done, then it would be difficult to change. I would still like us to stay open to possibilities. I've heard from some of you who don't think it's possible. Could I hear from one or two of you who think that it is?"

Emiko raised his hand. "I'd like to say that, while I agree that we get a lot of calls that are difficult to sell on, I can find about 20 calls a day where, once I calm the customer down and solve their problem, I can make a sale. I've learned a little bit more about their business and they're willing to talk about other needs. I've set a goal for myself to try to sell on at least 20 calls a day and have been exceeding my previous month's results."

Tim chimed in. "I've had a similar experience. I believe that I've earned the right to sell and taking care of the service issue first is non-negotiable. I take the opportunity to find out more about the caller's business, suggest a few ideas, ask if I can send them some information and arrange a call back. I spend about 90 minutes a day making call backs, and convert more than 50% of those calls into sales."

"Thanks for sharing your experiences. Before our next team meeting, I'd like each of you to keep a simple log. Just a 'T' with a tick mark on the left for calls that were too difficult to transition to a sale, or a tick mark on the right side for each call during which you were able to solve the customer's issue and transition to a sales conversation, even if it didn't result in a sale. In the meantime, I'll listen to some of your calls and see if I can hear anything specific to coach you on individually that might help you make the transition.

I agree that it is not possible on every call, but I would like for us to each be open to the opportunities that may be there."

We talked about a few example calls, and then I asked, if we could all agree to do this by our next meeting?

Reviewing the Development Process

Everyone nodded in agreement. I wrote this item on our action list. "This is a perfect transition to our next agenda topic, '*Reviewing the Development Process*'. I don't know what you've experienced in the past, but I plan to have a one-on-one discussion with each of you twice a month," I explained. "One of my supervisors did this with me, and I found it very helpful for both improving my job performance and career planning. I've created a worksheet for you that's similar to the one I'll use to plan our one-on-one discussions. It gives you some things to think about before I schedule time with you. I plan to keep these in your developmental folder, and use them month to month to see how you're progressing, as well as to help me know what you need from me to be successful." I'll be sending you each an e-mail to arrange an hour for our first discussion.

I passed out the Development Planning Worksheet.

STRETCH DEVELOPMENT PLANNING WORKSHEET FOR ASSOCIATES

What is the purpose of the development meeting/discussion?

_____

($+/\Delta$) What is going well? What would I like to be doing differently?

_____

Clearly describe the specific behavior(s) I wish to discuss:

_____

Address the effect of the behavior(s). What will happen if my behaviors change?

_____

What might get in the way of reaching my goals?

_____

Share realistic expectations. What specific actions do I want to correct/reinforce?

_____

Expected result identified. When? What are the consequences?

_____

How can my supervisor help me improve? What support or resources do I need?

_____

"The first objective is to be clear about what we each want to accomplish when we have our one-on-one time," I said. "It will be slightly different for each person, but the common theme will be career development and performance improvement. There will be other themes on the worksheet which will help you think about specific topics you'd like to discuss. We'll both share our thoughts at our meeting."

"Sometimes we may have different points of view on what needs to be worked on," I continued. "But that's why it's important for us to meet. If you have any questions about how to use the sheet, feel free to come to my office and ask!" I added *Scheduling one-on-one discussions* to our action list.

We had three more agenda topics, and we were a few minutes over the allotted time. I didn't want to skip any part of the agenda, so I moved ahead.

"The next agenda topic is '*Learn to Earn Skill*'. Again, this was a productive experience I had with another team. We spent 10 minutes sharing techniques that were helping us do our jobs better," I explained. "I've come prepared to share the first example today, and I'd like you to bring your ideas to share at future team meetings. It can be a technique that works for you, or a favorite phrase for positioning a product, or some idea that motivates you.

"Today I thought I'd share a quote with you," I said. "This is a quote I kept on my computer to help me remember to keep a positive attitude:"

"Selling is as much attitude as it is skill."

The whole team shared tips on how to keep a positive attitude. I then asked, "Does everyone understand the idea of the 'Learn to Earn' topic? I hope you'll take advantage of the time to share the ideas that work for you." I added *Bring a Learn to Earn item* to our action list.

Again, everyone nodded their heads in agreement. "OK, then let's move to the 'Open Microphone' portion of the meeting," I said. "This is your 'air' time to bring up any concerns or questions that are relevant to the whole team. It is not meant to be a time to solve issues, but to get them on the table. Does anyone have any concerns to bring up?" This is where I expected to hear questions about Charlie's dismissal.

The room went deadly silent. I looked around at each person, and they all avoided eye contact with me. Tommy finally spoke up. "I think Charlie's dismissal is on everyone's mind," he said. "We've all been talking about it since he was escorted out, and we have differences of opinion about whether he was treated fairly. I, for one, know that whatever he did must have been pretty serious to cause his dismissal. But we are all concerned about his son, and he still is a friend to many of us."

The tension in the room was like air on a humid day. "Tommy, I admire your courage to speak up on behalf of the group," I said. "I'm not surprised by your concerns or reaction. It was a very difficult decision. I can't divulge any details of his termination, but what we can do is review the memo from Human Resources about our code of conduct and ethics. I'm happy to talk with anyone privately if you have concerns with information discussed in the memo. I hope that each of you will be able to move past what happened and stay as focused as you can on your own performance."

I wasn't sure if that all came out right, but I was glad that at least it was on the table. "Are there any other open microphone issues?" I asked.

Esi piped up. "Yes, I've heard a rumor that we're going to be bought by another company. Is that true? How will it affect our jobs?"

Gosh, the rumor mill worked fast! "The supervisors met yesterday and the same rumor was raised," I replied. "Peter is getting clarification from our senior management and will share it with us as soon as he knows something definitive. I will make sure that I stay in the loop so you are informed as soon as we are. In fact, I'll add it to our action list."

Once I finished writing, I reviewed the action list. I then turned to the group and described the Plus/Delta process. I pulled up another blank flipchart page and began to write the group's comments.

PLUS

- *Liked icebreaker*

- *Eager for "learn to earn" skills*

- *Liked ground rules*

- *Intrigued by developmental process*

DELTA

- *Difficult topics, but glad they're on table*

- *Rushed—less topics or longer meetings*

- *Need snacks!*

- *Want sales and service goals resolved*

I thanked the group for their participation and adjourned the meeting, just a few minutes beyond the planned end time. As I walked out of the room, Emiko asked if he could talk to me. He sounded worried, so I told him to come to my office.

As Emiko sat down, he was twisting his hands nervously. He asked, "Could you verify what specifically caused Charlie's dismissal? I heard he was charging items on customer's credit cards that they hadn't ordered and was saying customers had to buy one product in order to use another."

I was not surprised by how accurate Emiko was. News usually travels fast, and many people were personally friendly with Charlie, including Emiko. I responded hesitantly, "Emiko, it is not appropriate to discuss any specifics about Charlie's leaving. If you have any specific concerns about how Charlie's leaving affects you, I would be glad to talk about them."

Emiko started to break out in a sweat. Whatever was going on sure had him worked up. He stated, "Well, I haven't done anything like charging credit cards without a customer's permission, but I have been positioning products as a bundle, offering a 20% discount if they bought both at the same time. I know that isn't the exact approach Marketing approved when they said we could offer a first-time customer a 20% discount, but I've had luck with this tactic. I just wanted to be sure that I'm not doing anything wrong and won't lose my job." He looked like he was going to faint as he wiped the sweat from his brow.

I decided I needed to say something quickly to get him calmed down. "Emiko, first, let me thank you for coming to me about your concerns," I said. "I know that Marketing has been somewhat flexible about how the 20% discount can be used to encourage first-time customers to buy. It may be a stretch to offer the discount to customers already with us, but I'm really not sure if it is inappropriate or not. I need to ask Peter and the Marketing group. I'll send an email and let you know the status of their reply by tomorrow. Then, I'll make sure we discuss the findings at our next staff meeting."

Emiko appeared to calm down. "I only used it if the customer hadn't purchased in a long time, or if they were really upset about a delay with an earlier shipment," he said. "I figured it was better to keep them as customers than let them go to the competition."

"Thanks for letting me know the details," I said. "It doesn't sound like you've been giving the shop away, and if it's keeping customers, Marketing may be willing to be even more lenient with their offer. I'd really like to get clarification before you do any more selling this way, though. I'll ask about it right away, and let you know as soon as I have some direction."

Emiko looked relieved. "I wasn't sure if you'd blow up about this or not," he said. "I'm glad you didn't and I'd be glad to show you the customers that I've extended the offer to. I watch their accounts closely to see if they come back to purchase other add-on products, and the majority do. I could pull the data for Marketing if they're interested."

"I'll keep that in mind," I answered. "Let's take one step at a time. If they seem open to the idea, I'll let them know they should talk with you. And Emiko, I admire your willingness to come to me today. I'm sure it wasn't easy."

"Thanks, Chris. I'm really glad it's off my chest." He emphasized, "I like working here, and I see a lot of opportunity."

Surprised, I said, "I didn't know you had career aspirations. Let's be sure we talk about your goals during our one-on-one time." As he stood up to leave, Emiko shook my hand.

This day sure had been interesting! It was almost time for me to close down my e-mail and make it to Lanie's game on time. I sent off an e-mail to Peter and Marketing about Emiko's concern. As I closed down my computer, I reflected on the day. I thought I had been quite productive and was very excited about the progress made in our first team meeting. I took my journal out and made notes so I would remember what to share with Stephanie.

- *Listening and asking questions helps clarify what's being said, and gives me a chance to think.*

- *I've got a great team!*

- *I think I handled the questions about Charlie without divulging confidential information.*

- *I stumbled when Charlie got defensive, so I need to work on remaining calm when someone gets defensive.*

- *I did not overreact and calmed down Emiko.*

9

Hiring the Right People

It was time to meet with Tiko to get a quick tutorial on hiring tips and to plan our interviews for the four candidates we'd be meeting over the next few days. I had jotted down some questions that I thought might work well in determining who would best fit my team. I realized I was really looking forward to working with Tiko, and learning some of his secrets for being a successful interviewer.

"Hey, Tiko. Is this still a good time for us to do the interview planning?" I asked as I stuck my head in his office.

"Hi Chris," Tiko replied. "Absolutely. I was just reviewing some notes from other interviews." He pulled out a chair for me to sit down.

"I jotted down some questions I thought would be good to ask as well," I said. "Where do we begin?"

Job Analysis

Tiko smiled. "I like to start by identifying the skills and competencies needed to be a team member. We had a job analysis done. It identified a standard set of skills required for the job," he explained. "I've learned that following a process ensures I'm fair to everyone. Knowing the strengths and weaknesses of my team ahead of time helps to keep my questions focused. When it comes down to two final candidates with similar qualifications, I focus on looking for the one who will best complement the team."

I was intrigued. I hadn't really thought about hiring from the perspective of who would add value to the whole team.

Succession Planning

"Now, that doesn't mean I always look for someone who is similar to the others," Tiko continued. "In fact, sometimes it is the exact opposite. For example, last year I had a team with very strong service skills, work ethic and follow through. They were almost a dream team. However, when I needed to replace Tonya, who had been promoted to the Marketing Department, I took a hard look at the group and realized that they weren't very savvy about long-term customer business needs. They also couldn't do the more analytical components of the job, so when I was doing succession planning, there really wasn't a strong candidate to be groomed for a supervisor role."

"How did you figure that out?" I asked, more fascinated than ever. "And what is succession planning?"

Tiko grinned. "Let me answer your last question first," he said. "Succession planning is important for the long-term growth, health and survival of the company. Each supervisor is asked to identify several associates who are best qualified and able to step into our shoes if we were to be promoted or leave the position for any reason," he explained. "We make sure we mentor and expose them to different opportunities to expand their knowledge and experiences.

"Like you, in fact," Tiko said with a wink. "When you showed an interest in various projects last year and thought of innovative ways to improve our work flow for storage units, it became apparent that you had some good supervisory traits. When Holly noticed you taking initiative, she mentored you. When the supervisory position opened up, she encouraged you to consider applying."

I remembered several conversations with Holly about my goals and ambitions. However, I never realized she was actually grooming me as part of a succession plan. As I thought more about how succession planning worked, I became puzzled. "Tiko, maybe I'm naïve, but couldn't the plan backfire?" I asked. "What if there wasn't a position open? Wouldn't that just cause tension and friction between the current supervisor and the person wanting to move up?"

Tiko thought a minute. "Well, I suppose that *could* happen," he said, "though I personally haven't experienced it. I think I've avoided it because I look at the overall character of a person, their motivation to move up, and their integrity. I look at how they handle themselves with others. I think, too, that it's all in how expectations are communicated.

"For example, I've been mentoring Lily, the other candidate who applied for your position," he said. "She's been working on different project teams and doing some of the number crunching for me. I encouraged her to apply for the job to get some interviewing experience. She learned from that experience and knows what she needs to do to become better prepared for the next open position, whether it is here, with another department, or even outside of this company."

I suddenly understood. "I get it," I said to Tiko. "It's not about a promise of a specific position, but preparation for when the opportunity presents itself."

"Exactly," Tiko replied. "So that's why it's important to look at the composition of the entire team and the needs of the organization. So now back to your other question—how do I figure out what I need?"

"Yes, this sounds important, but pretty complex," I responded.

"It can be complex," Tiko replied, "but I've broken it down into a few steps. First, I review the competencies for the customer associate based on the job analysis completed by Human Resources. They've provided us a common starting point, and then I can add specifics if I have any special needs. From a legal point of view, the skills have to be required for the job. Human Resources has also had applicants complete a pre-screening test for us, so we know the candidates we're interviewing possess some of the more 'hard-wired' skills we need, or those that are more difficult to teach. For example, they need the ability to empathize and self-initiate, and to possess predetermined levels of computer skills and writing skills."

Interviewing Approach

I thought about this. We're interviewing only candidates who have met our minimum requirements. But I still wondered how we prevented selecting poor performers. Tiko must have read my mind, because he added, "OK, so the next step is to prepare questions we want to ask each candidate during our interview. We have a standard interview form, with a rating scale that we will both use to help us be consistent with all candidates. It helps protect us from making biased decisions and also provides documentation in the event our decisions are ever legally challenged."

"What do you mean by 'legally challenged'?" I asked.

"Well, a candidate is protected by federal laws," Tiko replied. "For example, if we asked a question that discriminated based on age, race, national origin, religion or gender, the candidate could file suit. If that happened, we'd have to prove that every question we asked was job-related."

"Gosh, this is beginning to sound more complicated than ever," I said. "Maybe I shouldn't be doing this quite yet. Is there a class I could take to learn more about interviewing?"

Tiko smiled. "There are some awesome classes I'd encourage you to take that are very helpful Chris," he said. "However, we don't have the luxury of waiting until you've had the class. We need the bodies now. That's why we're preparing our questions ahead of time. I've made a copy of our standard successful employee profile, and I will guide you through the process, sharing my experience and thoughts."

I looked at Tiko. I had more and more respect for him and—remembering his great questions during my interview—I knew I could trust his advice. "OK," I replied. "Let's get this planning process going!"

Associate Competencies

I looked at the profile Tiko handed me. (See Appendix #2) It included a list of competencies, along with behavioral descriptions for both successful and unsuccessful candidates, using a 1-5 scale. There was an area for notes and comments. "Tiko, this list is really comprehensive. How do you use it for interviewing?" I asked.

Tiko pointed to the comments and notes area. "You're a step ahead," he chuckled. "I make copies of the same profile for each candidate we're interviewing. As I ask the interview questions, I make notes, or jot down key phrases used by the candidate as indicators of their abilities in a particular area. You'll do the same and, at the end of the joint interview, we'll compare our notes. It's important to understand and use the 1-5 rating scale." I reviewed the ratings and their definitions on the worksheet.

"I make notes and comments that provide evidence to support my rating," Tiko continued. "I prefer that we both conduct the interview together, alternating questions, and both keeping notes. We then share our impressions after the candidate leaves. Often, we may capture and hear a difference, which is why it's *critical* to have more than one person conduct interviews and make the hiring decision."

"Tiko, this sounds really helpful," I said, "but I don't see any sales-related competency. Isn't this a critical part of the associate position?"

Tiko explained further. "Well, sales experience is certainly important to the position. You'll notice that the behaviors that make a good salesperson are included in several of the competencies. For example, building relationships, being customer-focused, and possessing problem-solving abilities are among the skills of a successful customer associate. We can ask a specific question, such as 'Describe how you've sold a product or service to a customer.' We then listen to the 'story' they tell, and find out if what they describe exhibits those skills," he said.

"What is the FSTDO in the last column for?" I asked curiously.

"I've learned to interview for behaviors by asking questions that collect information about the candidate's past experiences, actions and accomplishments," Tiko replied. "I also probe for evidence of what they Felt, Said, Thought, and Did as well as the Outcomes of their actions. I put the first letters of each type of evidence to help me remember to ask further questions during the dialogue with the candidate to be sure I have enough information to make a fair rating. I also jot down what I've observed. Sometimes, when you're interviewing several candidates during a short time frame, who said what becomes blurred."

Interview Questions

"I still don't understand how to determine what questions are best to use," I said. "I made some notes from my coaching session with Stephanie, who said to ask questions to describe past performance, and you've stressed the importance of this too, but I still haven't figured out how to ask questions that make a candidate talk about the past. I did, however, come up with a few questions that I think are important."

I showed Tiko the questions I had jotted down. The first one was "Are you available to work nights and weekends?" "I think it's important to know availability ahead of time so there are no surprises when a new customer associate sees they've been scheduled for a Saturday or later shift," I explained. "I remember being surprised when I first took the job."

"Good question, Chris," Tiko said. "It can be asked because working Saturday or later shifts are job requirements. It can, however, be tricky, because you may be filling a day-only shift, and then the question could be interpreted as discriminatory. Your next question, 'What are your child-care arrangements?' is not appropriate because it could be interpreted to discriminate based upon gender."

"But it's such a problem when associates are late because of their kids, or it seems they're just so disorganized," I said. I remember being very frustrated by several associates who were chronically late because of sitter problems, shifting the work burden to others.

Tiko nodded and said, "Chris, I understand firsthand both sides of this issue, as well as the frustration it causes. I've found over the years that with a dedicated person with a strong work ethic, there are rarely chronic attendance problems. Of course, sometimes it's unavoidable. Questions about organization skills, work ethics and attitude can help us make a better judgment and identify the best candidate."

"Oh, I guess I see," I said. "This is really hard!"

Tiko nodded. "It gets a bit easier as you have more practice," he said. "Tell me a little bit about why you want to ask this last question, 'Are you a member of any clubs or social organizations?'"

I responded enthusiastically. "Several of my former team members are part of the International Technology Association. They seem to catch on more quickly to our products and services, to understand customer needs, and to be more comfortable building rapport and confidence with the customer. They seem to be the first ones to get the sales process down and bring in results," I explained.

Tiko nodded his head with interest. "That's a thoughtful observation. Let me suggest that we slightly reword the question, since the original question might lead to information about national origin, race, gender, age or other protected characteristics, and a candidate could claim that he or she was not hired due to discrimination," he explained. "If we make the question job-related, then it would be OK. You could ask, 'Do you belong to any professional or trade organizations that you consider relevant to your ability to perform the job?'"

I sighed, and then said, "I'm beginning to see how this works. As long as questions are specific to the job, we're pretty safe, right?"

"You're exactly right, Chris!" Tiko nodded with approval. "Now let's get down to asking other questions. I use the competency form to guide me, and write down any part of the candidate's answer that gives me observable, measurable actions that indicate they possess these competencies. I have a list of lead questions. These provide a starting point, and then of course, based on the answers we hear, we dig further for additional data. Here is a list of questions I've used in the past," he said as he handed me another paper.

I was amazed at how much planning and thought went into interviewing. I was beginning to realize that this was one of the most important things I needed to be proficient at. I rolled up my sleeves and began to read the list of questions:

1. *Define good customer service and describe an instance when you've demonstrated this service.*

2. *Tell us about a time you had to help a difficult customer.*

3. *Tell us about a situation where you had two associates not getting along and causing problems for the team.*

4. *Describe an experience during which you had to solve an issue. What was the final outcome?*

5. *Relate a time in your past when you had to sell or convince others to buy your product or idea.*

6. *Describe the management style of a former employer that you particularly liked.*

7. *Talk about a time when you participated in a project or task and were required to work independently. How and when did you receive direction? What did you do when an obstacle got in your way?*

8. *Give me an example of a good decision you have made in the last six months. Why did you think it was a good decision?*

9. *Tell us about a time when you received some constructive criticism. How did you feel about it?*

Tiko interrupted my thoughts. "Now, the next step is to determine which questions we each ask. That way, we know where we're going in the interview and, while one of us is asking and probing, it makes it easier for the other to be taking notes and observing the candidate's body language. After the interview, we compare key points from our notes and summarize them on the interview form."

"OK, how about you take the odd numbers, and I take the even numbers?" I suggested. "I think if you start us out, it will calm my nerves and set the tone of the interview."

Tiko wrinkled his face thoughtfully, and said, "This works for me as long as you don't present yourself in a subordinate role to me. Remember, we're both hiring one of these four!"

"Right," I said earnestly. "I'm still getting used to being in the supervisor role. And Tiko, I really appreciate all that you're sharing with me. I will take the next class on interviewing skills, but I think you've given me a tremendous jump start!"

"You're welcome, Chris," Tiko replied. "This is what teamwork is all about. I'm sure you'll return the favor soon when it comes to coaching and selling. I need all the help I can get in that area!"

I was surprised to hear this. I had the impression that Tiko had it all together. I looked forward to helping him in this area. I replied, "My pleasure, Tiko. I'd be glad to help you in any way I can."

Interview Ground Rules

"Thanks. Now let's move to the final stages of interview planning." Tiko continued. "Interviewing is a nerve-wracking experience, especially for a candidate who is not accustomed to this type of interview. I like to have an agenda so we use good time management skills, and it helps put the candidate at ease. I always tell the candidate that I'll be taking notes. A ground rule I also use is to make sure I give enough 'air time' to the candidate. I use the 80/20 rule of thumb, meaning the candidate speaks about 80% of the time, and I speak about 20% of the time. Here is a typical agenda I use," Tiko said as he handed me another sheet.

Interview Agenda

Welcome and Introductions
Review Agenda
Gather Information
Educational Background
Work Experience
Skill Evaluation
Company Information
Next Steps/Close

"I like to introduce each of us and explain our roles, and thank the candidates for taking the time to come in for an interview," he continued. "I try to put them at ease with brief small talk, and I make sure we use a conference room with a round table, so it doesn't feel like an interrogation room.

"I review the agenda, including the amount of time we have for the interview," he said. "This helps keep responses concise. It also tells the candidates what to expect during the interview.

"While I know each candidate's education from their resume and job application, I like to hear their description of their educational pursuits. This gives me rich insight about their goals, flexibility and work ethic," Tiko went on. "Then I ask about a major accomplishment in their prior job. This may not be relevant to the job at hand, but it gives us a wealth of information about their technical competence and their attitude toward work. Then we ask our behavioral questions to assess their competency and complete our rating.

"The next part of the agenda, Company Information, is our turn to sell our company to the prospective employee," he said. "It's a time when we're candid about the job demands, as well as the position, describing important aspects of the company that are attractive, yet accurate."

"Tiko, this is really helpful," I said. "I remember how my interview was conducted, and how at ease I felt once the agenda was reviewed. Stephanie gave me a hint to listen to the questions candidates ask because it is a good indicator of their interest in the job."

"I hadn't thought of that, but you're absolutely right," Tiko agreed. "I can often tell if a candidate has concerns or different ambitions when they ask only about salary or work hours. I'll make a note that we should add time for their questions to the agenda. Finally, I always like to let candidates know what will happen next. In this case, it's the final interview, so I tell them when they'll hear back from us and how they'll be notified."

"When do you think we need to have our decisions made?" I asked.

"Well, the sooner the better. The next new hire training class starts at the beginning of the month, so I'd like them hired before then. They may need time to give notice at another job, and I don't like to string candidates along. I usually like to make a decision within a day after the last interview which, in this case, is next week on Friday," Tiko said as he looked at his calendar.

"Wow, that's quick. Does that give us enough time to complete background checks?" I remembered that a background check was conducted on me when I first joined the company.

"Human Resources will have completed the preliminary check of educational status and employment history, and then it takes about another week for the criminal and drug check to come back," Tiko explained. "We hire a person with the hope that the check comes back "clean", but Human Resources emphasizes to never say "permanent" but that employment is based on the results of the completed background check information. Knock on wood, I've never had a problem."

"That about does it," Tiko said as he gathered his papers. "I'll get you a copy of this interview packet. We need to let Human Resources know our availability so they can schedule the candidates. How do the next two days look for you? We need about an hour per interview, and then a half-hour to complete our rating and discussions. I thought if we could interview all four in this week, we'd be able to make our decision before we go to our offsite meeting. I sure would like to have this task checked off my list!" Tiko sighed.

"I'm available except for my team meeting and a meeting I have with Natasha and Troy about the Cheat Sheet. How does 9:00 am to noon over the next two days work?" I asked.

"That works for me," Tiko replied. "I'll let Human Resources know and see if they can schedule the candidates that quickly. I'll let you know what they say. By the way Chris, I'm glad to have you as a partner on this interview. I am often concerned about the impression we give to candidates, because you never know if they may be a future customer or future employee down the road. I know you'll handle these interviews just fine!"

Smiling, I said, "Thanks for your vote of confidence, Tiko! And thanks for being a wonderful teacher."

I walked out of Tiko's office with a spring in my step. I felt well-prepared for the interviews and was now ready to tackle the action items from my team meeting.

10

Making Time Work for You

I couldn't believe how quickly the time went by. It seemed like there was so much I wanted to share with Stephanie and so many more questions. I pulled out my journal to prepare for our meeting, using the standard questions Stephanie had given to me.

- *What have I accomplished since our last meeting?*

  As I started writing, I was amazed at what I had accomplished and learned. I was most proud of the team meeting and getting a sub-team to work on the Cheat Sheet. I had met and involved the trainer, and I had a way to impact future new hire teams. I managed through the crisis with Charlie, and learned so much about interviewing during the planning meeting with Tiko.

- *What didn't I get done but intended to?*

  I improved a bit on managing time—at least I'd made it home before dinner every night. I didn't get all my team members scheduled for their one-on-one coaching session.

- *The challenges and problems I am facing now…*

  Getting ready for quarterly meeting; "fallout" from Charlie's dismissal.

- *The opportunity that is available to me right now…*

  Just staying on top of everything and spending time coaching my team.

- *I want to use my coach time to...*

Work on time management skills, and learn the best ways to develop associates.

I was ready for my meeting with Stephanie. She was working at her computer when I walked into her office. She swiveled around in her chair and said, "Good morning, Chris. It seems like a long time since we last met. How are things going?"

I could hardly contain myself. I told her all about the team meeting, and how the sub-team had worked together to come up with a final draft of the Cheat Sheet, as well as the steps to pilot it and measure results. She knew about Charlie's dismissal and its implications for me, but commended me on how I handled the team questions.

"How did the interview planning go with Tiko?" she asked.

"I almost forgot! It went really well," I said. "We've got the interviews scheduled for the end of this week, and I feel very prepared. Tiko is a super teacher and really knows his stuff. I'm sure I have more to learn, and I'm looking forward to working with him."

"So, Chris, where would you like to focus our time today?" she asked.

"Stephanie" I said, "I have two critical areas—my own time management and how I can best develop and coach my associates on their performance and career goals."

"These are significant areas. I can't think of two more critical topics. I have a 'hard stop' today, so let's choose one to tackle today, and then I can schedule an additional session with you tomorrow when my schedule lightens a bit," she suggested.

Personal Time Management

I thought a moment. I didn't want to shortchange either one. "Let's start with time management, because I think if I get that under control, the coaching will be more productive."

Stephanie replied, "OK, great. So let's find out where your time is spent. I'd like you to draw a circle on a piece of paper, and then divide it into pockets of time to represent how you spend a typical day. Estimate the number of hours or partial hours you spend on activities."

She listed on her board:

- *Sleeping*
- *Working at work*
- *Working at home*
- *Watching TV, reading, movies, leisure*
- *With family*
- *With friends*
- *Household chores*
- *Eating*
- *Exercising*
- *Other activities*

"Let's do a quick review of your day," she said. "What would it look like?"

I drew my circle. I wasn't surprised by the amount of time I spent working and sleeping, but I was surprised at how *little time* I spent exercising or doing leisurely activities.

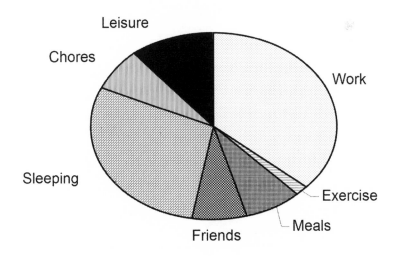

Professional Time Management

Stephanie looked at my drawing and said, "This gives you a quick snapshot to show how you spend your time. You may wish to draw the circle just for work, or just for leisure, or by the week or month. Draw one more now that shows how you spend time at work. What are the activities that you spent time on over the last week?"

I thought about the last week and listed these activities in my journal:

- *E-mail–10%*

- *Planning time–5%*

- *Reading reports–15%*

- *Team meetings–20%*

- *Listening and coaching live calls–20%*

- *Listening to recorded calls–5%*

- *Projects (Cheat Sheet)–10%*

- *Journaling–2%*

- *Eating–2%*

- *Individual team member questions–5%*

- *One-on-one development sessions–6%*

Stephanie continued, "After you repeat the circle activity several times over the next few days and weeks, ask yourself these questions:

- *Would I like to change the slices of time?*

- *What would my perfect circle look like?*

- *How can I change the size of some slices?*

"What strikes you as areas that you need to change?" she asked.

I first looked at my daily circle. "Hmmm," I paused to think. "I definitely need to take a look at increasing exercise. I'll bet I'll need less sleep if I do that."

"Exercising is quite important, especially to help you manage stress and to give you some quiet time for thinking. I've found that if I exercise, I feel better about all the other aspects of my day," Stephanie commented. "How do you think you can make the shift to move toward that goal?"

"I've been thinking about working out after work. By having that 'commitment' on my schedule, I think it would help me manage my time better. There is also a group in my neighborhood that runs together early in the morning before work, which may be another option—if I can drag myself out of bed."

"The one thing I know about making change happen is that you've got to take a bold step, immediately. What's one bold step you can take to start exercising more regularly?" Stephanie urged.

> *"To make change happen, take a bold step, immediately, and then do not look back."*

> *Used with permission from Dr. Sidney B. Simon, Professor Emeritus, Psychological Education, University of Massachusetts*

"I see your point," I pondered. "I'll stop at the community center on my way home and see how I can sign up. I think I'll start with either a class or personal trainer. If I know myself, I'll need the commitment of meeting with someone to keep me motivated."

"That's a wonderful idea. I look forward to hearing how it all works out," she laughed, "no pun intended. Now let's take a look at your time spent at work. What's one area you think you could change there?"

I looked at my work circle. "I'm surprised at how much time I'm spending reading reports, and how little time I'm spending working directly with my team associates. My intention at the beginning of the day is always to spend more time with them, but it always seems to get shoved to the end of the day."

Stephanie empathized. "Well, Chris, my experience is that *all* new supervisors struggle with time management, especially in the beginning. I think that coaching associates is the job-critical task for supervisors, so I'm always encouraging them to find ways to increase coaching time. In fact, I recommend that you spend 50% to 75% of your time on the floor with your associates. Here is an interesting way to see if there are any time wasters that are a part of your day."

Stephanie handed me a worksheet. "Take a quick glance at these and check the statements that apply to you."

INTERNAL TIME WASTERS:

Failure to delegate
√ *Managing fires/crisis*
Lack of plans
Doing the easy rather than the important
Procrastination
Failure to communicate
√ *Inability to say "no"*
√ *Fatigue*

EXTERNAL TIME WASTERS:

Telephone
Meetings
√ *Interruptions*
Mail and reading materials
√ *Lack of adequate information*
Television
Waiting time

I checked off several and said to Stephanie, "I think clutter is probably my biggest time waster. I have everything filed in piles on my desk, so when I go to look for information, it takes me forever to find it. I really like that my team feels comfortable to stop by and ask questions, or ask for input in handling a call. These seem like important interruptions, and I think they would fall more into the category of coaching. I hope this crisis regarding Charlie's departure won't be common, although we're down two full-time staff on our team, so it could heat up as everyone else is trying to pick up the slack."

Stephanie pondered, "If you could save one hour a week by arranging your files and eliminating the clutter, that's four hours a month, which could certainly be used more wisely with your staff. Would that be worth the investment of your time to get it organized?" she asked.

"When you put it that way, it makes a lot of sense to invest the time to organize things," I said. "I just have never been good at keeping everything in a place where I can find it. Have you got any suggestions?" I asked.

"This is really a personal preference" Stephanie replied. "I can tell you what works for me, though, to give you some ideas. I like to create general categories, like team meetings, reports, and staff meetings. Then inside the folders I either file documents chronologically or alphabetically. I also like to have a section of a file drawer devoted to housing folders for each employee, containing both electronic and hard copy documents. That way, anything specific pertaining to them goes in their folder and it makes it easier to do performance reviews when the time comes."

"Those are important ideas," I replied.

"Remember, Chris, one bold step is what it takes. What's the first thing you can do when you get some time at your desk?"

I drummed my fingers on the desk as I thought about what I could do. Then it came to me. "I'll go get some file folders on my way back to my desk. I can easily create a folder for each employee, and file each of their monitoring sheets in them. That'll clear off one whole section of my table," I chuckled. "From there, every time I need to look for a piece of paper, and find it, I can make a folder. By the end of the week, I should be able to create a filing plan so I can find them again."

"Those are both excellent ideas. How about writing them in your journal as your action items to complete before we meet again?" Stephanie encouraged.

I wrote "organize paperwork" in my journal, and then turned back to Stephanie. "I've got it noted."

Stephanie added, "Now, I'd like to share a few tips with you on how you *think* about time that I learned from Dr. Merrill Harmin, author of "The Quality Time Way to Go". He calls it the 'Go', 'NBA' and 'Do/Get/Be rules' to dancing through daily life."

I was intrigued. "I'm all ears," I said.

Stephanie began, "'Go' means we decide to act on something, or do nothing which, of course, is also doing something. In some way or other, we go ahead with our lives. To get what we really want, we have to first Notice, which is what the 'N' in 'NBA' stands for. We might be walking down the hall, thinking of our next meeting, when we suddenly notice that our shoulders are tense, or that a person in the hall looks lost."

I listened as Stephanie continued.

"We then get ourselves in better Balance, which is what the 'B' stands for. I might choose to shake out my shoulders, or just dismiss the tension as unimportant. I might pause to ask the person in the hall if I can help, or I might dismiss my concern, clear my mind and keep walking. Deciding what will keep me in better balance is how I make sure my time is spent in a meaningful way. Are you with me so far?" Stephanie paused.

"Yes, this is making sense," I said. "For example, yesterday I noticed that Raj was looking really puzzled and deep in thought, so I decided to go up to him and ask if I could help him. It turned out that he was trying to figure out how to enter an order on one of our new forms. I showed him how to do it in about two minutes, which saved him many moments of frustration and, likely, prevented a fulfillment mistake."

"You've got it," she said. "You decided that you and Raj would have better balance by taking the time to respond to his concern. Finally, the 'A' stands for Aim Ahead, or select targets to aim at then adjust as everyday events occur. When there are no goals, then we're often in reaction mode. We end up conforming to what others do, or what they don't do, rather than living a more self-directed life."

"I see. So aiming ahead is like targeting what's next. Even if our goal needs to be changed, we at least know what plan we're amending," I said.

Stephanie smiled. "You are exactly right."

I must have looked confused because Stephanie said, "As you aim ahead, you can track what you want to 'Do', what you want to 'Get' and how you want to 'Be' in the process. Let me explain further. Let's take your goal of getting your paperwork organized. That's your 'Do' and what you want to 'Get' is more time, feel more satisfied and have more order in your life. In the process, you choose how you want to 'Be', so you choose to be happy, positive, motivated, or you could be crabby, negative, aggravated. How you choose to be is how you will experience what you do," she said.

"Stephanie, it seems so simple, yet this is a big change in how I usually approach things. I'll give it a try in my daily planner," I said as I wrote in my journal to put a Do/Get/Be next to each item.

Stephanie continued. "Chris, you're already ahead of the game to have a daily planner. Let me show you one more way I organize things in my planner that I learned from Dr. Harmin. You can steal any ideas that might work for you."

Stephanie then opened her day book and showed me the section dividers:

- *Days*

- *Weeks*

- *Months*

- *Goals*

- *Reminders*

- *Supports*

I was really curious, since I'd never seen a day planner organized in this way. Stephanie said, "My new goal is to get this into an electronic version, but it'll be easier to show you how it works on my hard copy."

She went on to explain that she used the A-Z like a personal encyclopedia. She had names, addresses, phone numbers, but she departed from the usual alphabetizing by putting her Auto mechanic under "A".

"Wow. How long did it take you to set this up?" I asked.

"I've been doing it this way for more than two years, based on a time management class that I went to when I first started my coaching job. I wasn't very organized either so, you see, there is hope," she joked.

"It wasn't this filled up at first," she continued. "I transferred to this year's planner what I wanted to continue to use from last year. It has saved me a ton of time trying to locate information. I know just where it is, and it makes it easy to keep track of everything important to me. Let me show you the section on months."

She turned to the monthly calendar, with appointments, holidays, birthdays and other commitments noted. "I turn to this section first when I'm planning to see what's coming up. You'll see that I have more details on my day calendar," she said, turning to the next section. She showed me how our coaching meetings were on her daily calendar.

"I put my goals and reminders in the next sections. These are longer term goals and projects. They get broken down into smaller steps which are then written in my monthly and daily to do lists. For example, here is a long term goal to become a certified Master Coach." She pointed to a note written in her "Goals and Reminders" section. Flipping back to last week, she showed me how she had one task each day related to achieving her goal. For example, on Tuesday, she had listed "30 minutes researching on-line classes".

"My favorite section is the support section, where I put favorite quotes, letters from others that cheer me up, photographs of my kids, jokes that make me laugh. It got so big that I had to make a whole folder, which I pull out when I need a little motivation."

I was amazed, but didn't know if I could become quite that organized. "Stephanie, I think these are superb ideas, but I already don't seem to have enough time to do what I need to do. These all seem like they'd take even more time!"

Stephanie empathized with me, and said, "Oh, Chris, I don't expect you to create a daily planner all at once. I just wanted to expand the way you think about time, and show you some alternatives. Start by putting the sections together that will work for you when you have some energy. I already see that you are a list maker and know how to put priorities to your tasks.

"At the very least," she continued, "I strongly encourage you to take 10 to 15 minutes at the end of each day to plan for the next day. For example, plan for some of the interruptions, and leave some time for those so you don't feel like they're interruptions. Investing in planning your time will pay off in having more time for the things that are important to you."

As Stephanie closed her day planner, we almost said in unison, laughing, "Making change happen is taking a bold step, immediately!"

"Stephanie, I'd like to at least write down the areas you're suggesting and give them some thought," I said. "I like many of the ideas and, as I organize my papers, I already can see how some of these sections will help me." I quickly wrote the sections in my journal and starred the support pages and the A-Z encyclopedia.

"Chris, we're at the end of our time today. May I schedule you for some time tomorrow so we can discuss coaching tips?" We compared our calendars and chose to meet early the next morning.

11

The STRETCH Coaching Model

The next morning, I arrived at Stephanie's door promptly at 9:00, and met her coming down the hallway. "Come right in, Chris. I was just getting a second cup of coffee. It was a late night with an overtime soccer match for my son's team."

"I can certainly relate," I chuckled "because Lanie's team has played two games for each of the past two weekends to make up for rainouts."

"So, we're meeting this morning to talk about coaching, right?" asked Stephanie.

"Yes," I said. "I want to streamline how I coach my team so they can exceed what they're doing right now. I have a few naysayers on the team but I think that, when they taste a small dose of success, they'll be willing to give it more of a try. I just need to make sure I come up with a way for them to be successful."

"As you might have guessed, Chris, this is one of my favorite subjects. I think of coaching as unlocking the potential of each person you manage. I use the word STRETCH to help keep my own coaching focused toward this goal. Let me show you on the board what each letter represents, and how to use them as a coach."

I copied what Stephanie wrote on the board into my journal:

S▶T▶R▶E▶T▶C▶H: THE COACHING PROCESS

Set the Climate   _____

Target Needs and Goals   _____

Review Alternatives and   _____
   Promote Discovery

Explore Possible   _____
   Solutions/Consequences

Talk/Agree on Parameters   _____
   and Next Steps

Confirm Scope of   _____
   Responsibility/Follow-up

Help Obtain Resources   _____
   and Summarize

Stephanie turned around from the board. "You'll notice, Chris, I gave you the first two steps of the process at an earlier session. They were, just to refresh your memory "*set the climate*" and "*target your needs and goals*". Have you had a chance to use them with your team?" she asked.

Enthusiastically, I replied, "Yes. In fact, they really helped me put together my team meeting agenda and I've begun to use them with a planning process I gave out to each team member to help prepare for our one-on-ones." I pulled out the form I had passed out during the last team meeting.

STRETCH DEVELOPMENT PLANNING WORKSHEET FOR ASSOCIATES

What is the purpose of the development meeting/discussion?

_____

$(+/\Delta)$ What is going well? What would I like to be doing differently?

_____

Clearly describe the specific behavior(s) I wish to discuss:

_____

Address the effect of the behavior(s). What will happen if my behaviors change?

_____

What might get in the way of reaching my goals?

_____

Share realistic expectations. What specific actions do I want to correct/reinforce?

_____

Expected result identified. When? What are the consequences?

_____

How can my supervisor help me improve? What support or resources do I need?

_____

"Holly used to use this for my one-on-one's and I found them very helpful," I said.

Stephanie laughed. "It's delightful to see that my coaching is paying off. Holly and I created this during one of her coaching sessions a few years ago when she was struggling with how to communicate expectations with her team members. I'm glad to see that it worked, and that it's getting recycled!

Unlocking a Person's Potential

"Let me explain the other parts of STRETCH," she continued, "and then I can share a few other handy work sheets for you that Holly probably didn't show you, since they were for her planning."

Stephanie explained that "*setting the climate*" was important to create a mentally, emotionally and physically positive environment. "This puts people at ease and establishes your credibility with them. The focus is on building rapport, resulting in strong trust, which you need for teamwork," she said.

I explained to Stephanie the icebreaker and ground rules we had come up with during my first team meeting. "Those are perfect examples," Stephanie exclaimed. "Trust is built by listening to different perspectives, sharing decision making, sharing responsibility, and collaborative feedback. There is also a way to help your team members take responsibility for their own development. Here is a quick little 'quiz' you're welcome to use as you start your one-on-ones. I created the quiz after reading a book by Master Coaches Judy Feld and Ernest Oriente which reinforced the importance of being open to and understanding the role of coaching. The quiz helps to introduce your role, but also stresses the expectation that each person is ultimately accountable for their own development and progress."

Stephanie handed me a sheet of paper from her files. "You're welcome to make all the copies you need, as long as you have a conversation with each person when you use it."

"I promise" I said, with a twinkle in my eye as I looked at what she handed to me.

S▶T▶R▶E▶T▶C▶H: HOW COACHABLE ARE YOU?

Select the number that comes closest to representing how true
the statement is for you right now and fill in that circle. This test helps
both the coach and you discover how coachable you are right now.

1= Less True   3= Moderately True   5= Very True

I can be relied upon to be on time for all calls, appointments and coaching sessions.	☐ 1 ☐ 2 ☐ 3 ☐ 4 ☐ 5
This is the right time for me to accept coaching.	☐ 1 ☐ 2 ☐ 3 ☐ 4 ☐ 5
I am fully willing to do the work and let the coach do the coaching.	☐ 1 ☐ 2 ☐ 3 ☐ 4 ☐ 5
I keep my word without struggling or sabotaging.	☐ 1 ☐ 2 ☐ 3 ☐ 4 ☐ 5
I'll give the coach the benefit of the doubt and "try on" new concepts or different ways of doing things.	☐ 1 ☐ 2 ☐ 3 ☐ 4 ☐ 5
I will speak straight (tell the whole truth) to the coach.	☐ 1 ☐ 2 ☐ 3 ☐ 4 ☐ 5
If I feel that I am not getting what I need or expect from the coach, I will share this as soon as I sense it and request that I get what I want and need from the relationship.	☐ 1 ☐ 2 ☐ 3 ☐ 4 ☐ 5
I am willing to stop or change the self-defeating behaviors that limit my success.	☐ 1 ☐ 2 ☐ 3 ☐ 4 ☐ 5

www.callcentercoach.com

Stephanie said, "You'll notice from the way the 'T' is highlighted in the word STRETCH that this is all part of targeting goals. You targeted team goals, and the worksheet helps get individual goals articulated. There is a saying: 'If you don't know where you're going, you'll never know when you arrive.' Naming what success looks like, and the specific actions needed, is often how a coach helps clarify goals."

"I think this is where I get stumped, Stephanie," I said. "I see what they should be doing, but they don't seem to buy into the ideas if I just tell them what to do. I don't know how to get them to identify their goals, quickly. How do I do that?"

"You've just put your finger on one of the most difficult, yet most important, skills a coach brings to the table—the art of asking questions," Stephanie said.

"Questions?" I asked.

"Yes, questions." Stephanie replied. "Questions help individuals sort out what they're thinking and also can help them focus forward. Let me give you an example. Consider these two questions and how the answer to each will create a different result."

Stephanie wrote two questions on the board:

- *What's the problem you're having with closing sales on your calls?*

- *What HAS been working for you to close sales, and what's one issue that is causing you difficulty?*

I sat and read the questions to myself three times. "What do you think?" Stephanie prodded.

"Well, if you asked me the first question, I would be defensive, thinking that you think I'm doing a lousy job. And if I don't know how to do something, I really can't put my finger on what it is, kind of like a blind person trying to describe something they've never seen. The second question doesn't put me on the defensive."

"In fact," I said, "it makes me really think about what I am doing well, but gives me the chance to describe a problem so I can obtain help in discussing solutions."

"Bingo. You've got it," she said. "So the lesson here is that you need to engage individuals in targeting their goals, and ask questions that are *forward-focused*. The worksheet that Holly gave you, and you've now shared with your team, does exactly that. Now here is your part of the planning worksheet."

She handed me a sheet that looked similar to the one Holly had used, with some specific differences. It was designed to elicit *my thoughts* as the coach about where to focus the coaching discussion.

S ►T►R ►E► T► C► H: DEVELOPMENT PLANNING

Worksheet for Coaches

What is the purpose of the development meeting/discussion?

_____

_____

($+/\Delta$) What is going well? What would you like to be done differently?

_____

_____

Clearly describe the specific behavior(s) you wish to discuss:

_____

_____

Address the effect of the behavior(s). What are your reactions to the behavior?

_____

_____

How do you think the person will respond?

_____

_____

Realistic expectations shared. What specific actions do you want to correct/ reinforce?

_____

_____

Expected result identified. By when? What are the consequences?

_____

_____

"Chris," Stephanie remarked, "It's important to "*review alternatives*" while you're discussing new goals. Sometimes when we're learning new information, or have done things the same way for a long time, a coach can help reframe the issue so innovative solutions can be found. You can simply ask the question,

'What other options might there be?' and of course, there is no better way to build someone's confidence than your willingness to adopt someone else's ideas."

"But how do you get from identifying alternatives to making an actual decision?" I asked, puzzled.

"Good question. The STRETCH process helps you get to the point of a decision. When you *explore pros and cons*, you're taking an all important step by looking at the potential impact of each solution before implementing any. It's not foolproof, but it does help prevent failed attempts, and makes for better decision making all around."

"I'm sorry, Stephanie, but I'm not getting this step," I said. "How will a person know the pros and cons if they've never attempted something?"

"Think about it this way," she said. "Let's say a person's goal is to learn how to drive. They've never done it before, but they really want the freedom to be independent. The pros might be that they'll fulfill a dream, they know they can work with an instructor who has done it a thousand times, they can wait and choose a day with ideal weather to practice, it'll give them a way to get back and forth to work so they won't have to worry about the bus being late, etc. The cons might be that it's too much of a risk, they don't have the money to pay for an instructor with the amount of experience they'd like, they're too afraid of bad weather to drive, bus fare is cheaper than buying a car, etc. By weighing the pros and cons, it helps to see the whole picture before a decision is made."

"I see now," I said. "The pros and cons aren't about the actual driving, but about the goal of learning how to do so."

"Yes, however, once they've learned to drive, they may have a new goal—for instance, driving to an out of state destination. Then the process starts all over again." Stephanie explained.

She continued to describe how important it was to *talk often and agree on the next steps* "By having very specific, small baby steps, we gain a sense of accomplishment, but the dialogue is critical, too. Remember, as individuals take their first steps, they can become discouraged or lost."

"I certainly can relate to this," I concurred. "Holly would often have to rope me back in when I first started working on the escalation team. I would almost want to drive to the customer's site to make sure they had their problem resolved. I was going overboard on all customers, and she showed me how to identify which customers to spend more time on."

"Holly is an effective coach," Stephanie replied. "She's worked very hard and been with the company a long time. Over time, she has refined the coaching process to make it work for both the customer and company. In fact, she is among the best to confirm expectations and goal parameters."

I must have looked perplexed, because Stephanie said, "The bottom line is that if you don't confirm the scope of a goal, it gets out-of-hand and can often overwhelm and paralyze. Action plans become very important."

Action Planning

She turned to her file system and pulled out a piece of paper. "Here is a tip sheet that has come in handy for me for action planning."

Always specific

Concrete   *Prevents confusion*

Timed   *Limit scope*

Immediate   *Agreed upon*

Owned   *Now!*

Necessary

"Whenever we're working with individuals on a goal, or coaching them as they take on a new project, I encourage them to use this checklist to ensure success."

"For example, let's say a goal is to learn to ask better questions during a sales call. You want to always be specific about what constitutes better questions, providing concrete suggestions. You don't want the learning to take forever, so you start immediately with an agreed upon end time. You need to be clear about why improvement is necessary and limit how much behavior can be changed at once."

"Oh," I interrupted, "So, if I want someone to learn a new process with twenty steps, I shouldn't give them all twenty at once. They wouldn't be able to remember them all, let alone perform them."

"Exactly right." Stephanie replied. "A coach helps identify what's most important, and helps the learner stay focused until proficient. You want small successes to keep a person motivated. The individual's accountability needs to be clearly defined and owned. By adhering to these steps, confusion is avoided and everyone is on the same page about what has been agreed to. Starting immediately on an action plan makes it become a reality."

"Oh, OK. I am clearer now. Break it down into manageable pieces," I said. I explained that it was similar to what my daughter's soccer coach was doing. The team is learning how to pass the ball this week, and that's all they've been focusing on. Last week, they practiced different ways to dribble the ball with their feet. Some of the girls wanted to do both at once and their coach clarified that next week they'll put the two together, but until they're proficient at each, it won't be as successful. As I finished describing this, I said, "I can see the same thing at work here when I coach associates on how to move from service to sales. My motto will be *one lesson at a time and action plan!*"

"That's a terrific motto," Stephanie said. "Remember, Chris, the action plan is also important when facilitating a meeting. Following these same criteria help to clearly define desired goals and assign accountability."

I thought about this for a minute. Stephanie was right. I had participated in many meetings where fantastic ideas were discussed, but nothing ever happened or got implemented.

Stephanie interrupted my train of thought. "Coaches also help others by connecting them to and "*helping them obtain resources*" they may need to acquire—like training, tools, information from other departments, and people in the call center—these all help minimize obstacles as they learn new skills."

Stephanie pointed out how she had already been using many of these steps with me, and how we'd continue to use the process during our coaching relationship.

"Stephanie, this is beginning to all make sense. I do have one burning question, though."

"What is it, Chris?" Stephanie said with concern in her voice.

Providing Feedback

"I really like the STRETCH process, but what about when I have to give feedback? It's not always about being nice, is it?" I asked.

Stephanie grinned. "No, it's not exactly about being nice, but rather being clear and positioning information in a way so the other person can hear the message's intent. We've got a few more minutes before I need to get to another meeting, but I think this will help answer your question, and give you some guidance around giving feedback."

As she turned back to the board, she said, "All feedback is positive when delivered with care. The feedback is *received* with care, as well, when it's tied to a developmental goal that you've discussed. I use the word CARE to help me remember how to stay positive."

She turned to the board and jotted down the letters CARE, with a description following each letter:

Clearly describe behavior

Address reactions to the behavior

Realistic expectations shared

Expected results

"Let's say that you need to let someone know that they missed a sales opportunity," she said. "You need to put your finger on a measurable, observable behavior they didn't use so they can understand what they need to do differently. For example, they missed the opportunity because they didn't clarify and review with the customer what was said and needed. That would be the behavior you describe. And you want to start out positively. It could go something like this," she said as she wrote on the board.

She drew a quick diagram, and filled in the blanks with an example:

S ▶T▶R ▶E▶ T▶ C▶ H: CARE MODEL
GIVING/RECEIVING FEEDBACK

Clearly describe behavior	Sue, I'd like to share with you a technique that helps me determine if I have a sales opportunity. Try summarizing what the customer said was needed.
Address reactions to the behavior	This will let the customer know you heard their needs, and position you to offer one of our solutions.
Realistic expectations shared	Try saying something like: "Mr. Customer, I understand you're having a difficult time managing your inventory, especially during your busy season. Is that correct?"
Expected result identified	I often write down key points the customer makes during the conversation so I can remember the points to review. I'd like you to give it a try, and I'll check back with you to see if you've been able to increase sales during your calls."

"Wow. This is exactly what I've been missing! Thanks for letting me know about the CARE method of giving feedback!" I said.

"You're welcome. I want you to know that it can also be used to praise someone for a job well done. How about if you write down a few examples that you use before we next meet, and we'll see how it's working for you?" Stephanie suggested.

"Good idea," I said, as I added it to my journal list.

The phone rang. "Chris, this is my next meeting," Stephanie said. "This was an excellent session. See you next week!"

She picked up the phone and asked them to hold for a minute. "Oh, I almost forgot that I'm not here next week. I'll e-mail you with a few options for the following week. I think you've got plenty to keep you busy!"

"OK, I'll look for your e-mail," I said. "Thanks again."

I left Stephanie's office, reviewing the STRETCH worksheet and committing it to memory. My tool kit certainly had grown during the past couple of days. Now, I just needed to put all these techniques to good use.

12

Strategies for Team Building

It was the morning of our quarterly manager meeting. I was running late since Lanie had missed the bus and I had to take her to school. I rushed to my desk, grabbed the materials that Natasha, Troy and I had worked on over the last few days and the agenda Peter had sent yesterday, and started to walk over to Rose's Cafe.

I was proud of the work Natasha, Troy and I had completed. We received good comments from a few associates who tested the Cheat Sheet and had already made some modifications based on their input. I put the finishing touches on the rollout plan last night so we'd be ready to share it with all of the supervisors. I sure hoped everyone would give it a fair chance.

As I walked, I wondered what I would learn from the exercise that Stephanie had asked all supervisors to complete. It had taken me a long time to think of my answers. It would be interesting to hear the results.

Tiko, Holly and David were walking just ahead of me. As I caught up to them, they were talking about Quinn coming to our meeting. I had not had a chance to look at the agenda, or my morning e-mails, so they quickly filled me in. Peter had sent an update late last night indicating that Quinn was going to join us for the beginning of the meeting. We all began to wonder if the rumor about the merger was true, and if that was why she was attending.

When we arrived at the meeting room, the rest of the team members were already there. Natasha handed me a folder with copies of the Cheat Sheet. "I made a copy for everyone, Chris, along with a summary of the results from the first round of associates" Natasha said.

"Oh gosh, thanks for making the copies. I had totally forgotten about them!" I added them to my folder, and thought to myself that it sure was nice to have others on the team pulling some weight!

As I grabbed a glass of juice and a muffin, the door opened behind me. Peter was with Quinn and they were deep in conversation. Everyone moved to the tables and sat down. As Quinn started setting up a computer and screen, Peter said, "Good morning everyone. Thanks for being here promptly. We have a very full agenda, so I'd like to get started. As many of you know, we have a slight modification to the agenda, as Quinn came to my office late yesterday afternoon to brief me on the rumor about the merger. We both thought it best that she be available in person to update you and answer your questions."

He handed out the revised agenda which included Quinn's update, reviewing the results of the employee satisfaction and customer satisfaction surveys, team building with Stephanie, and reviewing the Cheat Sheet and Weekly Tally. It sure was a packed day; I was glad to see there was time scheduled for lunch!

Communicating Mergers

Quinn stood up and thanked us for squeezing time into our agenda for an update about the merger rumors. She confirmed right away that the rumors were correct and that Power Solutions would be merging with Watershed Designs by the end of the year. We listened intently as she displayed several slides noting significant goals and time lines.

"It is critical to understand and communicate that this merger will *double* the size of our company along with our product and service offerings, and that Power Solutions' senior management will be at the helm of coordinating the union," Quinn stressed. "It is equally important that you and our staff understand that *no one*, I repeat, *no one*, will lose their jobs as a result of the merger; rather, we need everyone's support to make each phase successful. Our plan is to keep growing the business, and Watershed Designs fills a gap that we've had in our product lines."

The room was quiet as everyone absorbed the news. Peter said, "This is the time to ask any of your questions, especially those you anticipate from our associates."

Susan spoke up. "Quinn, I was here when the last merger happened. I understand all of the positive benefits; in fact, I'm intrigued by the products and services you described that we'll gain from the merger with Watershed Designs. My concern is that we take our time and do it right."

"Last time our systems didn't catch up with what was promoted for months," she continued, more deliberately now. "We had two separate ordering systems; we gave the associates no time to adequately train on the new computer screens, let alone become familiar with the features and benefits of the new products and services. It caused many good associates to leave our company, and was a very stressful time for all of us!" she concluded emphatically.

Quinn replied. "Susan, I've heard the stories about the last merger, and believe we've learned from our mistakes. In fact, we're looking for representatives from each level of the organization to be on the merger planning and implementation committee. I'll be leading the effort. Perhaps several of you would consider joining us?" she asked, looking around the table. "It will be on top of your regular responsibilities; however, I think you would agree that we'll all benefit in the long run."

"I was discussing with Quinn on the way over here that this is a tough time of year to take additional time away from daily activities," Peter interjected. "However, I believe it is critical that we have representation on the team, so I'm going to make a personal commitment to be a part of the process. I will leave it up to each of you to determine if you can handle adding one more thing to your plate." Turning to Quinn, he continued, "I think that there will be many more questions as the days go forward. I know this group is especially concerned about how we'll be informing our associates. Could you comment on the communication plans?"

Quinn smiled. "If there is anything we learned from last time, it is that we have to keep everyone informed, even if we don't have all the answers yet," she said. "I'll be participating in different meetings all day today and tomorrow, reviewing the same information as I did here today. There is a memo going out to all employees before noon today, outlining what we know so far, with a hotline number to call with questions or concerns. We'll be publishing a weekly update on e-mail once the planning committee is under way so everyone knows what's been accomplished and what still has to be decided. I expect there will still be some surprises along the way; however, I hope that you will help to keep the lines of communication open."

I looked around the table at my colleagues and noticed that Natasha was about to raise her hand. Peter said, "Natasha, do you have a question?"

"Yes, I do," Natasha replied. "Quinn, I heard you say that no one would lose their jobs. Will employees of Watershed Design be joining us?"

"That's a good question," Quinn answered. "Right now, Watershed Design has two call centers, one on the east coast and one on the west coast. One decision that needs to be made is whether there is an advantage to moving everyone to this location, or whether we should keep all three sites going. Our real estate department has been assigned to take a look at the impact of lease agreements, the cost of offering jobs and moving people. There are also some questions about our hours of operation. Right now, we are open from 8 a.m. to 8 p.m. Eastern Standard Time. However, we'll be getting many customers from the west coast, so we'll need to be available for them."

David piped up, "If we have longer hours, will we have more shifts?"

"That's a possibility," Quinn replied, "but it's way too soon to say specifically what will happen."

After several other questions, Quinn concluded with these remarks. "Your questions are all excellent, and I encourage you to keep asking them. I want to underscore how important it is that your employees are also encouraged to ask questions and to use the process we've laid out to get answers to their concerns. We want to do this right, so the transition is as smooth as possible."

Peter thanked Quinn for her time, and she said, "If any of you have further questions, please let me know, and of course, if anyone is interested in being on the committee, you should let Peter know no later than next Monday."

After Quinn left, Peter said, "Rather than wait for associates to ask us questions, I'd like to be proactive and solicit their concerns. So, let's agree on a bulleted list of critical points to review, and then commit to have a team meeting with your associates to discuss them within the next few days. I know that we can't all be off the phones at once, but I would like to squelch as much of the misinformation that the rumor mill has created before it gets out of hand."

We spent the next fifteen minutes discussing the key points to share during our team meetings. As we were winding down, Susan said to all of us, "These are important points, but I don't know how we're going to pull teams off the floor, and keep our queue of calls managed. Shouldn't we just send out a memo?"

Peter responded strongly. "We need to check with Scheduling to see what can be done to get every team off the phones for at least 10 minutes. It's difficult to judge whether they understand the message when we're not there to see their reaction, and it's important that they are comfortable from the start asking questions and getting answers," he said.

I saw Peter's point, and made a note to see when I could fit in a 10-minute meeting. Then, I spoke up. "I am concerned about everyone getting consistent information, especially as we learn more each day. What if we have a 'before and after hours' question and answer session, so anyone with burning questions has a forum to get them answered?"

Everyone was quiet, and many looked uncomfortable. Finally David spoke up. "Chris," he said, "we've tried that before and the associates felt they should be paid if they have to come to a meeting outside their regular work schedule. The same people show up, while others don't bother."

"Oh, I see." I shrugged my shoulders, and asked, "What if we at least offer the option, rather than make it a requirement?"

"I don't think it would hurt to try it again," Tiko chimed in. "The last time we tried it was when we made changes to the commission scale, so everyone was already in a confrontational mood. I say let's see what happens this time around, as long as we still have our team discussions and an e-mail update. We've never tried either of those before, so I think having several opportunities for discussion and information sharing is a good thing."

Peter jumped into the discussion. "I see all of your points and I think the idea is worth trying," he said. "I'd also like to keep track of the questions being asked, along with the answers. Everyone filters information a different way, so we need to be as consistent as possible. Since there are five of us, I'd like each of us to facilitate the discussion one day per week. I'll send a daily update to each of you with any new questions and our answers. Likewise, if any issues come up, I need to know what they are so we can give a thoughtful response. Is everyone in agreement?"

We all nodded our heads and then Peter wrote our names by a day of the week so we'd be ready to start the next day. "Let's see how this works for a couple of weeks, and then we'll modify it if we need to," he said.

Responding to Customer and Employee Feedback

Peter continued, "This was a great discussion, and I know that we'll work together when the merger comes. Let's turn our attention now to the present. I have the results from our customer satisfaction and employee surveys. I e-mailed them to you all late last night, but in case you didn't get a chance to download them, I've made copies for each of you.

"Let's first take a look at employee satisfaction." Peter proceeded to hand out thick packets of paper that included the results from both surveys. On the front cover of each was an executive summary.

"We'll focus on the executive summary," Peter said, "but if you need more information, the backup data that supports the summary is included in your packets. Now, Sarah from Business Analysis will give us a quick summary of the results."

Sarah turned on her computer and began showing us the results. She began discussing interesting correlations, as well as what was important to employees and their satisfaction.

First, she described how the data had been collected. It was clear that the employee satisfaction results had come from our annual employee survey, which every employee across the organization had completed, including non-call center employees. What we were looking at was a report comparing call center results to the rest of the organization. The results were depressing. The rest of the organization was at a 48% satisfaction level while the call center was at 32%.

Peter turned and said, "When I first saw these results, I was as surprised as you are. We've been working hard all year to make changes based on last year's feedback. I've concluded that, while we have work to do, we can't wait for a year to see the impact. I've sent an e-mail to Marketing to request that they conduct a shorter survey to measure results in those areas we decide to work on.

"There are two reasons for this," he continued. "One is to know very quickly if our efforts are giving us the desired outcome, and second, to raise awareness that we are proactively addressing concerns. I don't think we've been very proactive at letting our associates know that their input has influenced the changes or decisions we've made."

Troy looked at Peter and said, "Will we be able to see our individual results? I'd like to know if I'm dragging the group's results down."

Implied in Troy's comment was to see *who* was dragging the group down, and everyone knew it wasn't him. All eyes turned to Peter. I wondered how he was going to handle this comment.

"Well, let's all be certain that we don't assume that any *one* person has total impact on the results," Peter replied quietly. "I will be meeting with each of you individually to show you your specific scores; however, not one of us here can ignore the issues that are blatantly in need of improvement. We all own the total picture, since we all interact with each other and influence what goes on here."

Troy was blushing, and red splotches were creeping up his neck. "I..., I'm sorry," he stammered, "I hadn't intended to imply that—I guess I wasn't thinking."

Peter accepted Troy's apology. "OK, then," he said, "let's continue."

Determining Focus

"Let's determine what needs to be done to turn this around for the next survey," Peter said. "I'd like to do a quick multi-vote to determine where we should focus our discussion time."

He asked each of us to select a symbol to represent our name, wrote the symbol next to our names, and then listed each of the survey items on the board, from lowest to highest satisfaction. He said each of us could use our symbol five times to vote on the issues we thought could have the most impact with some focused improvement effort. If one of us felt strongly about a certain issue, we could use all five symbols on it, or we could divide the symbols however we'd like, as long as we used a total of five, and no more than five. Once we posted our ratings, Peter said he would show us how the associates had rated each issue.

△ = Troy   √ = Susan   □ = Tiko   + = Chris   ♥ = Natasha   ▀ = David

Supervisor Rating of Potential Impact		Associate Rating of Importance
△ □ ▀	Decision Making	
△ □ □ + + √ ♥	Coaching	
+ ♥ ▀	Communication	
△ +	Work Schedule	
√ ♥ ▀ ▀	Training	
△ ♥ √ ▀	Appreciation/Recognition	
♥ △	Stress Level	
	Call Monitoring	
□ □ √	Supervisor	
+ √	Career Opportunities	
	Pay	

It was very interesting to see where everyone thought we could improve employee satisfaction. Judging by the higher rankings, it certainly was clear that the group agreed that Coaching, Training and Appreciation/Recognition were important "need" areas to target.

Then, Sarah showed us a fascinating chart displaying the most important issues for our employees.

Supervisor Rating of Potential Impact		Associate Rating of Importance
◊ ◻ ▪	Decision Making	6
◊ ◻ ◻ + + √ ♥	Coaching	1
+ ♥ ▪	Communication	4
◊ +	Work Schedule	10
√ ♥ ▪ ▪	Training	2
◊ ♥ √ ▪	Appreciation/Recognition	3
♥ ◊	Stress Level	7
	Call Monitoring	11
◻ ◻ √	Supervisor	8
+ √	Career Opportunities	5
	Pay	9

I was not surprised to hear that they thought coaching was important. I was stunned to find that, for our employees, training, appreciation and recognition, followed by communication, career opportunities, and, finally, decision making from the management team were other top concerns.

Peter remarked, "When performance is viewed against importance, we can see the "low hanging fruit" and it becomes immediately obvious where to focus our first efforts."

We had a lively discussion comparing our top choices with the choices rated most important by employees. Both groups agreed that appreciation/recognition and training were priorities. "I think communication from management is on everyone's mind because of the pending merger," Natasha pointed out. "We already agreed earlier in the meeting that communication is part of our action plan. I think, if we focus our resources on coaching now, we'll be in a better position later to address their opportunities." We continued the discussion, narrowing our future focus.

"Based on this discussion," Peter summarized, "it sounds as though we should focus on the areas of training, coaching, and appreciation/recognition."

He then asked us to form three groups, assigned a "need" area to each and asked us to brainstorm action items for improving employee satisfaction. We were encouraged to open the packet to understand the data behind each of the final scores.

Initially, we quietly read the report in more detail. I paired off with Holly to work on Coaching. I was glad to have the chance to work with her, since I really admired her analytical abilities and how she turned them into practical action items. Her coaching skills were also top notch, so I was sure she had some valuable insight. Plus, I might have a chance to ask her about the MBA program she was taking from the local university.

I opened the packet, looked at the specific statements around Coaching and found three references to issues pulling the employee ratings down. The first was *"The support after training has prepared me to do my job well."* It wasn't a surprise we scored so low, since we'd already discovered that many associates were struggling to include service and sales in the same call, and the new product information was coming out more quickly than it could be absorbed.

We scored 36% on the next statement, *"There is clear communication from our management."* I had heard many complaints from my own team that not everyone knew what was expected of them. Changes were frequent, and there were often mixed messages about what was most important—service, sales or productivity. My guess was the communication about the last merger had caused much confusion also.

The third statement, *"I am appreciated for my contribution to the enterprise"* scored among the lowest of the entire survey at 27%. I knew that we rarely had time to celebrate successes, and when we did have time to coach, we emphasized needed improvements, rather than praise.

As I shared these thoughts with Holly, she pointed out some other statements which also had low scores. *"My coach is available to help me with difficult customers,"* and *"I am comfortable asking my coach questions about how to improve my sales."*

"I'm intrigued with how many of the low scoring statements are related to doing well on the job," Holly said. "The implied good news is that our associates want to do well if we just give them the right tools at the right time. I'm actually pleased to see that even though communications are an issue, our ratings have improved since last year. But we sure have a lot of room for improvement!"

"But isn't *attitude* as important as tools?" I replied. "I mean, if you really want to do a good job, don't you eventually figure it out?"

"Sometimes, but why make it more difficult than it has to be?" Holly said emphatically. "Let's see what we can come up with for solutions."

We continued brainstorming until Peter called time. As we turned to rejoin the larger group, Holly said, "I'm taking a class right now and we're studying how employee satisfaction can predict customer satisfaction. I'm curious to see what Sarah has to say about our customer satisfaction results."

I whispered to Holly, "That *does* sound very interesting. By the way, when we get a few moments, I'd like to hear more about the classes you're taking!"

"I'd be glad to tell you about my graduate program," Holly said. "I'll warn you though, it's very grueling to hold a full-time job, go to school at night and still have a life. But I am learning tons of new information, or at least ways to look at things a bit differently."

As we reconvened, Peter opened with an interesting thought, "I think our ability to coach and communicate is closely correlated with employees feeling appreciated." With that encouraging thought, Peter then asked each group to share their ideas and recommendations, while he summarized on the board:

Training

- *Include 45-minute refresher training in team meetings.*

- *Integrate evaluations into training to identify who is doing well/needs help.*

- *Have a peer mentor process with high/low performers.*

- *Devise on-line key word search for product knowledge.*

- *Invite research and development staff to discuss how products and services were designed to meet customer needs.*

- *Invite customers to share product/service benefits.*

Appreciation/Recognition

- *Offer more meaningful incentives, rather than just dollars, i.e. days off, special parking spot near the building, etc.*

- *Have a peer-nominated incentive for helping each other that costs little, i.e. paper hands hung from tree with helper's name.*

- *Share publicly positive customer feedback.*

- *Have a system in which points can be earned and traded for gift certificates to local establishments.*

- *Have a group of employees devise a reward package.*

Now it was our turn. Holly and I alternated sharing our list.

Coaching

- *Take administrative duties from supervisor to free up time for coaching.*

- *Set minimum expectation about time on the floor spent coaching side by side with associates.*

- *Offer training on how to effectively coach.*

- *Hold coaches accountable for team/individual improvement.*

- *Share examples of model calls.*

- *CARE model (I shared Stephanie's thoughts).*

- *Have supervisors practice to improve confidence.*

- *Create a process to track coaching results.*

- *Tie coaching into development plans.*

- *STRETCH (I shared Stephanie's ideas).*

As Peter asked us to take a look at the board, I realized there were some incredible ideas up there. They all appeared like they would work, although it seemed a bit overwhelming to try to do them all. I wondered which ideas I would be most comfortable trying out. Peter's voice pulled me back from my day dreaming. He asked us to pick the ones we could effectively accomplish *and* would have the greatest impact at the most reasonable cost to the company. This was a tall order, but I should have known by now that this group of supervisors loved a challenge!

Tiko jumped right in. "I really like the idea of including 45 minutes of training on our weekly agendas," he said. "We could take turns coming up with the 'lesson of the week' based on what our monitoring observations are indicating we need to improve."

Susan nodded enthusiastically. "I agree, *and* I'd like to suggest that we," she motioned to the supervisory group, "develop a method to know *how* we're doing. Currently, we don't really keep track of individual strengths and developmental needs, so we're not really focused on improving our own performance in key areas."

David looked like he was struggling with these ideas. Peter recognized this and asked for his opinion. "David, it seems like these aren't sitting as positively with you? What are your thoughts?"

"It's not that I don't like the ideas, but I really think we first have to take some administrative responsibilities off our plates," David replied. "I, for one, don't know where I could find one more minute for more documentation, or even expanding my team meetings. Maybe I'm missing something here, but it seems like we're being a little too optimistic."

Tiko said to David, "I'll bet you are feeling overwhelmed now because you own all the reporting, you just had three associates leave, and with the new baby and all… Anyway, I don't think any of us can start these things immediately, but I do think we should consider them as options for the future and have a plan to get there. Don't you think?"

"Well," David paused, thinking. "I suppose you might be right. As long as I won't be held accountable to do all of these things right away, I might be able to take a few small steps at a time."

"That's a good point, Tiko," Peter said, adding "David, we really haven't agreed yet to what we'll do, although once we agree to take action, it will take some adjustment on everyone's part to change. I would like to continue this discussion, though, and agree as a team on three action items we'll work on. The Marketing Department can conduct a mini-survey to test the impact we're making."

Holly spoke up. "Shouldn't we involve, or at least ask, our associates their opinion before we go ahead and agree on actions?" she asked. "While many of us have done their job in the past, the expectations have changed quite a bit. I always have better luck getting their buy-in when I ask them to help come up with a solution. We'd also be communicating that we listened to their feedback and want their input."

Peter nodded. "That's a really critical consideration, Holly. I'm certainly anxious to get these scores changed and moving in the right direction. Why don't we simply agree on the three we're most comfortable with, and then ask a group of employees to join us at a planning meeting to come up with the specifics for accomplishing the tasks? They can let us know if these actions would have the most impact, and if not, we can amend our agreement from today. How does that sound?" Peter looked around as we all shook our heads affirmatively.

"Alright," he continued, "then let's firm up what three action items we'd like to propose to the associates—one from each category." The three we thought had the most potential were:

- *Increase coaching time on the floor using the STRETCH process and CARE feedback model.*

- *Include 45 minutes of refresher training in each team meeting, using various teaching techniques.*

- *Encourage associates to form a group to develop a point system for incentives.*

Tiko, Troy and David were asked to take the lead on pulling the incentive planning group together. Holly and I were to put together a schedule for coaching leaders on the floor and review the STRETCH model and CARE feedback guidelines; and Natasha and Susan were assigned to work on the refresher training schedule and resources. I was also asked to take the lead on the interim marketing survey. "This is a big step in improving our employee satisfaction results," Peter said. "Let's now focus on what our customers are telling us. Sarah, can you first show us the survey results?"

Sarah brought the screen back up and said, "It's not surprising to see how closely correlated customer and employee satisfaction are. They are often predictive of each other. We asked a third party to survey our customers after they'd had an experience with our call center. It's the same company we used for our customer perception studies, but this time we really wanted to know only about the call center. We provided them lists of customers who had called in within 48 hours of their transaction with us. That way, the customers had total recall of what happened."

She drew a breath, and I sensed some bad news was coming. Then, abruptly, she smiled, saying, "Well, the news from our customers isn't so bad. We're performing better than the average call center, but about the same as our competition, and that is exactly what we need to change."

"As you know," she continued, "we are trying to differentiate ourselves from our competition by creating a 'wow' experience for the customer. With that directive from our President, this result is not good enough."

"OK," I said. "Can you define a "wow" experience for the customer, so we can train and coach to deliver it? I think I know what it is, but I'm not sure." There was an uncomfortable silence after the question. It didn't seem an easy question to answer.

"That's a provocative question," Sarah finally replied. "You know, to answer we should look at some of this feedback and see what drives our customer satisfaction, just like we did for our employees." She pulled up the same sort of chart we'd just seen, but clearly from the customer perspective. She reviewed the results, highlighting that our strengths were price in the market for our products, quick problem resolution, and outstanding quality of products. She noted that there were three key areas for improvement: associate knowledge about products and services, timeliness of fulfillment, and need for some additional products and services.

"All right," said Sarah, "here's the crunch. These high priority improvement areas are also those in which the call center is performing least well."

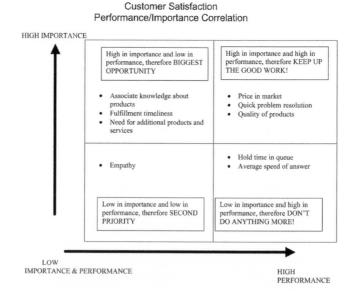

Customer Satisfaction
Performance/Importance Correlation

My head was swimming. Peter leaned back in his chair, seeming to process everything at once. "I get it," he announced. "There is really a clear story here. Our customers want the basics—give me what I called in for quickly, while showing me you care. Meanwhile our employees have gaps in their knowledge from either poor training or poor communication. If we fix these two basic issues, it should have an immediate impact on our customers."

"OK," I ventured, "but what about the 'wow' factor?"

Holly jumped in at that point, obviously very excited. "I think 'wow' is two things. Like Peter said—deliver what they expect each and every time, but deliver the message in a way that says we care about their business. Frankly, if our employees don't think we appreciate them and what they do for our company, why should they go 'beyond' to be warm and friendly?"

"I'm not surprised by the results at all," Susan immediately said. "Our escalation team has been doing a phenomenal job taking care of problems since we put them in place as a result of last year's survey, and we've always been competitively priced with the best products."

"I think our agreement to focus on training earlier will improve our associate's knowledge, but maybe it's more than that," Holly chimed in.

"It's a first-rate idea to better support our associates' product training needs," Tiko agreed, "but I think we have a bigger systemic problem in this area. Training does a superb job with what they have, but it would be valuable to have real products on display so associates could get hands-on experience using them. It's so hard to learn just from drawings and user manuals."

We all thought about Tiko's idea. "We've had discussions in the past about clearing space against the south wall and having our products displayed," Peter said. "But we needed the space, so we haven't done it."

"How about the large atrium as we enter work?" Natasha said. "It's certainly large enough and would even look good to the public. Our associates could rotate in and out and "test drive" the products."

I could visualize exactly what Natasha was referring to and said, "I like that idea. The atrium should be big enough, and it could become a display for the whole company."

Peter asked, "Does everyone think this would be a good place to bring employees and show our products?"

"Will it be big enough for new products and services after the merger?" David asked.

"Excellent point, David," Peter responded. "I'm not sure, but I'll take ownership of this one and bring the idea to Quinn and the senior managers to get their input."

We talked a few more minutes and agreed this seemed like the best approach, as long as training staff were involved in the process. It was added to the list as Peter's action item. "So that leaves us with the fulfillment complaints. Any ideas on how we might impact this one?"

Peter addressed Susan. "Susan, I know you're a part of the project team that is looking at fulfillment issues," he said. "Has there been any discussion about issues we create in the call center?"

"The only issue that has come up so far is that we need to be double checking for accurate shipping and billing information," she replied. "However, we've been analyzing root causes, and this contributes very little to the problem. The majority of the causes seem to be either systems or back order inventory related. I don't think we have a lot we can do to solve either of these issues."

"Thanks for the update, Susan," Peter replied. "I think we've completed our action items, at least for this time, on how to improve our employee and customer satisfaction results."

I piped up. "Peter, pardon me, but I have one more idea that I'd like to mention. Since we scored really well in problem resolution, and we're looking for ways to improve how we appreciate and recognize our employees, I think we should commend our associates on doing such an outstanding job in this area," I said. "Just having come from the floor, I know there has been quite a bit of focus on acting with urgency and resolving issues for unhappy customers. I remember learning that when we solve customers' problems and do a good job, they will more likely stay loyal to us. We always let our associates know when there are problems; I think we need to celebrate the wins when we have them."

"Chris, you're absolutely right!" Peter said with pride in his voice, "Celebrating is one thing we don't do often enough. I have an idea. I wonder if we should ask the new incentive team to come up with a way that we can celebrate. That way, we'll find a meaningful way to reward everyone."

Everyone nodded in agreement. Peter commended us for a provocative dialogue and subsequent actions and then moved us to the next agenda item: Cheat Sheet update.

Natasha, Troy and I handed out the final Cheat Sheet, the training outline we had prepared, and reviewed the results of the pilot group. "Did the associates say if a specific area of the Cheat Sheet worked over another?" Holly asked.

I looked at Natasha and Troy. We had heard quite a few comments about how helpful the questions were. "It seems that the most difficult area for the associates is to transition from their service solution to sales," I replied, "and they've told us that the questions suggested on the Cheat Sheet seem to be helpful. Our team has discussed their observations, and we see that this Cheat Sheet has helped them focus their questions. However, there are still many associates struggling with how to keep the conversation customer-focused and continue probing for other needs based on what they hear from the customer."

"I've been coaching my team to always resolve the customer inquiry before they transition to sales," Susan said. "This seems to make it clearer in their minds what comes first. They're learning how to use the same information they normally get during a call to identify what other solutions might be sold. They're getting really good at using the information as part of their transition statement. It just takes time and practice to refine these skills. I found having a focused conversation to be one of the skills that comes after time and experience. I'm confident that the idea we had earlier to have associates listen to high-quality calls will help, too."

"I have learned that the more comfortable my associates are with product knowledge, the easier it is for them to have a helpful discussion," Tiko added. "The individuals I observed using the Cheat Sheet during the pilot, who were previously struggling, were very complimentary about how this helped them stay focused, and their results show it! I'd say the sooner we give this to everyone, the sooner we'll see results. Are we now authorized to use it?"

Peter asked for everyone's commitment to give it a try and to begin tracking results and responses from the rest of the team. He then thanked our sub-team for our hard work and gave us each a gift certificate to the local mall. We were beaming with pride, and I thought to myself, "It sure is amazing what good teamwork can accomplish!" I was so glad that Natasha was a part of this accomplishment, and I had a feeling that her team was going to show the most positive results.

The meeting broke for lunch, and the rest of the team thanked us for our work. As we walked to the buffet table, Natasha stopped me and said sincerely, "Chris, this wouldn't have been successful without your patience and flexibility around my schedule. I want to thank you for showing me how we could get this done with each of us putting a little bit of time into it. I learned a lot from you about organizing information—and myself," she chuckled, "and I hope we get to work on another project together soon."

I smiled at her and said, "Thanks. I hope we get to work together again soon, too. I'm sure glad, though, that our presentation is over, and I can enjoy lunch!"

"I agree!" Natasha said cheerfully. "Let's eat!"

Peter called the meeting back to order after lunch. We had two agenda topics for the afternoon. Tiko was up next to present the Weekly Tally idea he'd been putting together to help us more efficiently manage reports and paperwork. Stephanie would then join us to conduct our team-building session.

Strategic and Operational Measures

Tiko began his presentation. "As I mentioned before, my previous employer used a tally to ensure its business objectives were being met. It helped us to look at the needs and expectations of customers, stakeholders and employees, as well as to determine how to measure our success and meet our goals. It helps to pinpoint what is working or not working."

The points Tiko made so far made sense to me and were beginning to answer my questions about how the data we collected was used to measure our success.

"Our company has several strategic measures in place," he continued. "I think it's important to know what they are and how they are used, since our operational measures impact them."

Tiko passed out a worksheet that listed the Strategic Measures, and he gave a brief explanation of each one. They focused on the operational measures that he was recommending we use to manage our daily work. Tiko went on to explain that, while all of the metrics were somewhat interdependent, he felt there were several indicators that we as supervisors had more direct control over.

Strategic Measures	Operational Measures
Customer Lifetime Value ($)	Service Quality
Share of Wallet (%)	Sales Productivity/Team Items Sold Per Order $ Value Per Order
Retention (%)	Adherence To Schedule
Penetration Ratio (%)	Average Handle Time
Customers Highly Satisfied	Occupancy
Conversion Ratio/Sales Channel (%)	Service Level
Revenue Per Conversion	Customer Satisfaction
Cost of Sales per Number of Leads ($) per Conversion Rate	Sales Revenue
Service Level (%)	Employee Retention/Positive Attrition
Cost Per Service Encounter ($)	Coaching Sessions Per Associate
Highly Satisfied Employees (%)	Employee Satisfaction
Shareholder Returns	Return on Equity

"I know that we hold associates accountable for their average handle time, as well as occupancy, adherence to schedule and after call work time," Tiko said. "I've always been uncomfortable holding them accountable for service level, too. When calls are in queue we 'sound the alarm' for everyone to jump on the phone and we make them feel like they need to rush through their conversations. I think service level is more a function of how we schedule our staff, how we use our Interactive Voice Response system, how we route calls, and the available trunk lines."

David spoke up. "Tiko, this looks like more areas to measure than what we have now. I thought our goal was to streamline the number of reports," he said with exasperation.

"David, I agree that there are a few more measures here," Tiko responded. "However, this Tally Sheet is one sheet that summarizes what is important for each of us every day. Right now, we get six different reports, which require us to wade through so much paper that there's no time to act on what we've learned! Personally, I'm spending more than two to three hours a day just reading them from my e-mail attachments and making sense out of them. I'm proposing that we have one person manage the data and put out this daily report. I think we'd all be more productive, and we could then focus solely on improvements."

Peter jumped in. "Tiko, what you're saying makes sense; however, we can't really add to head count until we get through the merger planning."

Tiko looked disappointed, but not defeated. "I thought that might be the case. What if we reorganize a bit? Maybe we could temporarily free up one supervisor to do this job entirely, if we disbanded his or her team and divided it among the rest of us. The other supervisors could take on an extra two direct reports and then one supervisor would be available to pull the numbers together?"

Everyone seemed to be thinking about this unique approach, when Susan responded. "I could handle a few more associates if this report was handed to me every day," she said. "It would be difficult to get to each of them for coaching, but I'm willing to give it a try."

"I don't think I could handle more than I have right now," Natasha said, "even with less paper work. And I'm not sure it would be fair to the associates, either."

Then Holly said thoughtfully, "If I had 15 associates, I could spend an hour per week with each person, and have enough time left over for project work and all of the other responsibilities. What eats up my time are meetings and unexpected tours that we're asked to give."

Directing his remarks to the entire group, Peter asked, "How would you feel if we stopped doing reports for a week, and kept a time log on how we're spending our days? I did this recently and found I had more than four hours a week that I was wasting, and have begun to change my habits."

We all looked at each other. I spoke up, "If we're not looking at any reports, then how will we know if we're in trouble?"

"I'm willing to take that risk," Peter said emphatically. "Since most of us are plowing through the reports now, with little time left over to take any action, I think by focusing on the floor more, we'll know more quickly what is going on. I'm not sure we can do the associate shift, Tiko, but I'm willing to find someone from our quality team who can help put this report together. We could ask them to monitor just enough calls so each of you would have trend information. If they monitor fewer calls they should have time to pull reports."

David practically stood up and cheered. "I already like the idea," he said. "Any day without the drag of getting all of these reports prepped is a better day for me!"

Peter then postured, "If everyone will make the commitment to keep a time log next week we can eliminate two to three hours per day of report reading and, instead, direct our attention to the floor. Then we can see what the impact is during our next staff meeting. Do we have consensus?"

While there were mixed feelings about it, everyone agreed to give it a try for a week. Peter thanked Tiko for his work and recommendations and then suggested we take a break.

Personality Styles

When we came back into the room, Stephanie was setting up in front.

Peter called us back to order, and Stephanie explained that she would be showing us our individual and team results of the feedback survey, and how we could best work together. She stressed that this exercise wasn't about labeling us, or fitting us into a specific box, but rather to learn more about how to take advantage of each other's strengths.

She explained that we should each read our profile, which described our interpersonal communication style. She then showed us a grid of our team profile on the board and said, "Each of you have a touch of all four styles: Helper, Initiator, Organizer and Thinker. I put your name in the quadrant where you scored the highest. Let's begin an exercise intended to give a deeper appreciation of each other's gifts." She pointed toward the board:

Quadrant A: HELPER   **Quadrant B:**

                                      1

                     Holly

          Susan   2

                                      3   Natasha

                                      4

                                      5   David

INITIATOR 1   2   3   4   5   6   5   4   3   2   1 ORGANIZER

                                      5

                                      4   Peter

          Tiko   Chris   3

                                      2

                                      1

     Quadrant C   THINKER   **Quadrant D**

Stephanie continued. "The good news is that this is a very diverse team, which can really help you look at issues from different angles. Because you have such differences, it can also get in your way if you don't understand how to use each other's strengths. The next few exercises are designed to help you learn more about how to best work together. Does anyone have questions before we begin?"

No one had any questions, so Stephanie continued. "The first step is to learn about your strengths. Some of you fall in the same quadrant even though you may have different strengths. For those of you in the same quadrant, I'd like you to do this exercise together. I've put an A, B, C and D on four different flipcharts around the room. I'd like you to take your chairs and move to the flipchart that corresponds to your quadrant on the profile."

Holly and Susan went to Quadrant "A", David and Natasha went to Quadrant "B", Tiko and I joined each other in the Quadrant "C" area, Peter went to Quadrant "D."

Once we were settled, Stephanie continued. "Now I'd like you to draw a "T". On the left side, list adjectives or phrases that describe you. On the right side, list the challenges, or how your style might bump into the other styles. Use the profile description I've given to each of you to give you some ideas."

This is what the lists looked like:

Strengths A Challenges Holly and Susan		Strengths B Challenges David and Natasha	
• Get things done	• Too emotional	• Attention to detail	• Very cautious decision maker
• Loyal	• Temperamental	• Plan for future	
• Patient	• Looking for recognition	• On time	• Everything is black or white
• See possibilities in others	• Heart rules head	• Objective	• Don't function well in chaos
• Offer support	• Need acceptance	• Prepared	• Don't challenge rules
• Compassionate		• Follow rules	
• Peacemaker		• Dedicated	
		• Dependable	• Judgmental
• Takes action	• Aggressive	• Quiet	• Head rules heart
• Adaptable	• Make own rules	• Sees the big picture	• Complexity in relationships
• Good in crises	• Rebellious	• Likes to learn	
• Don't like to wait	• Too impulsive	• Looks at all possibilities before making decisions	• Indecisive
• Need choices	• Don't anticipate problems		• Aloof
• Quick to make decisions	• Like the spotlight		• Uncaring
• Spontaneous			• Too abstract
• Independent		• Competent	• Too independent
Strengths C Challenges Tiko and Chris		Strengths D Challenges Peter	

Once the lists were done, Stephanie asked us to share them with the group. I was fascinated as I thought about how each person interacted within the group. I recognized how others reacted to me, and how I reacted to them.

"Let's use an example to see how we can either play to our strengths, or let our differences get in the way," Stephanie said. She pulled a bunch of puzzle pieces out of an envelope and asked us to work together to put it together. Holly and Susan began to move the puzzle pieces around to see if they could fit them together. David spoke up and asked, "Do we get a clue as to what the puzzle is about?"

"It's something that is important to all of us," Stephanie answered.

I jumped in and suggested we try to put some of the same colors together, so we moved the puzzle pieces around. Tiko started working on a section of one of the colors, while Natasha followed with a different color. Peter looked at the puzzle and said, "I'm not convinced that all of the colors go together in one area. We need to get the edges put together and then we'll have a better idea how the colors are arranged."

What a good idea! We all began to find the flat-edged pieces and Holly began to put them together, with David joining in. Peter was right. Once we had the frame of the puzzle completed, it began to go together quickly.

We looked at the finished puzzle, and Stephanie asked, "What do you think the puzzle represents?"

"It looks like people riding different types of unicycles," Tiko said.

David chimed in. "Yes, and I see a dollar sign on the bottom right, and a gear on the middle one, and the top one looks like a multi-colored wheel."

"And it looks like they are riding on different paths, but they all touch each other," Natasha added.

Stephanie nodded her head and smiled. "You're all very perceptive. The artist was asked to draw a representation of how people, processes and work flow intersect with individual strengths to meet bottom-line results. What you've just experienced is exactly that. We can lean on each other's strengths, and still share different perspectives as we communicate and make decisions."

This was interesting, but I wasn't sure I was totally following Stephanie. She continued. "We each can use all of the styles if we choose to. However, our first reaction will usually be to use what is within our comfort zone."

"But isn't labeling each other detrimental to our work?" exclaimed Holly. "I don't really like being put into a certain 'box' or expected to react a certain way all of the time."

"You're exactly right, Holly," Stephanie replied. "This is only meant to help us be aware of each other's strengths. We all have abilities in all the areas. For example, let's assume in the puzzle exercise, Peter thought of his idea to put the frame together first, but he remained quiet. If this were the case, we'd want someone to ask for Peter's input."

Holly said, "I see. So it doesn't mean that I get labeled as too emotional or temperamental."

"No, but it does signal others that they should pay attention to you and check in with your concerns," Stephanie explained. "Let's say the team has a project that will have a big impact on the business. It would be important that David and Natasha be consulted to see that the plan has all of the details in it to make it successful, since that is their strength. Holly's and Susan's compassion should be tapped to ensure impact on staff is considered; Tiko and Chris will push the group to closure if it gets stuck; and Peter will make sure that the plan fits the big picture. Do you see how this example uses everyone's strengths?"

"I initially had the same reaction as Holly," Susan replied, "but now I see the point. I see how important this is going to be when we work on the merger."

"We actually use each other's strengths quite well," Peter added. "Look at how Tiko and Chris came up with the Cheat Sheet, and we all added our thoughts on how to make the implementation work. We did the same in thinking of how to improve our satisfaction results. I think what this does for us is give us another tool to use as we move toward being a top notch team."

Stephanie continued on with Peter's thoughts. "Exactly, Peter. It is a tool, and it gives us a common language to use as we seek others' input. It also helps us be more attuned to each other's needs and reactions so that we can all be more supportive. Finally, you can 'borrow' styles by watching others and using them as a model to strengthen your own tool kit."

"Stephanie, thank you for sharing this tool with us," Peter said. "I know that our team will put it to good use." Stephanie acknowledged our thanks and left the room.

Peter said, "I promised everyone we'd end on time, and we have just only our plus/delta to complete. Who would like to start?"

Tiko said, laughing, "I'll stay true to my style and get things going. I think a huge plus is that we accomplished a lot in one day, but I feel energized rather than tired."

"I'd second Tiko's comment," Susan added, "and add that I'm really glad we're getting input from our associates on the incentive plan, and secondly, our action items seem realistic and also seem like they'll make a difference."

David said, "And I'm thrilled that we've at least started to see how to improve our measurements and reporting process!"

Peter flipped it around, "Any deltas?"

"I'd be more comfortable if we had a clearer plan for the merger committee, and who will be on it," noted David. "I'd like to suggest that we decide that at our next staff meeting."

Holly laughed. "Thank you David, for keeping us organized!"

He responded with a chuckle. "At your service anytime!"

We finished the plus/delta and Peter adjourned the meeting. I was overflowing with so many things I learned today. I decided I'd jot down a few notes in my journal before I called it a day:

- *Be aware of my natural style and how it works.*

- *Look for examples to "borrow" from other styles.*

- *Communication is a cornerstone to success.*

I then wrote in my planner to conduct a 10-minute meeting tomorrow to discuss questions on the merger. I also added a note to lead the merger discussion Wednesday morning.

As I packed up to leave, my head was filled with different aspects of the day. I was very excited to be leading my team over the next few months through the changes that were coming. I reminded myself to ask Stephanie about tips to help them manage change.

Like Tiko, I, too left Rose's Cafe Restaurant with a sense of purpose and energy. I marveled at how well Quinn, Peter and even Stephanie turned around what could have been a miserable day.

13

How to Slide Uphill

It had been several weeks since our quarterly staff meeting and my last meeting with Stephanie. Information about the merger was common knowledge, and our communication process was working, even though there had been a few glitches along the way. We had to make some adjustments to get the latest information to everyone.

It was Tuesday afternoon, and my next meeting with Stephanie was scheduled for tomorrow morning, so I wanted to spend some time getting prepared. Stephanie had been assigned to the merger planning committee, so she now had even less time for coaching, and I wanted to make the most of our meetings. She had assured me that meeting with me was still among her top priorities.

I pulled out my journal to look at the questions Stephanie had given me to prepare for our coaching session, and began to think about my responses.

- *What have I accomplished since our last meeting?*

  This was a long list. I had made progress in managing time better, but I still found it challenging to leave work on time and fit in more exercise. I had spent two hours per week with every one of my associates, so their development plan was completed, and I was sitting by each person during their calls to help them. I was getting very good at using the CARE model in giving feedback and was receiving compliments from some members of my team. The Cheat Sheet was producing results and, surprisingly, it was showing our teams' product knowledge gaps. We now had a product display in the atrium, and the

144

Training Department had started to revamp new product training. Tiko and I had completed our interviews and made hiring recommendations for the open positions on our teams. Our new team members were in the midst of learning the "ropes" of the job and exhibited some promising talent. I still had one more job opening. A friend of mine mentioned that he had applied and asked if I would put in a good word for him. I wondered if I should interview him.

- *What didn't I get done but intended to?*

I had promised Tim from my team that I would spend extra time coaching him on calls but, so far, I hadn't been able to squeeze it in. I had also promised Lanie I'd make her home soccer games and had missed two.

- *The challenges and problems I am facing now…*

Even with all of the positive things going on, several individuals on my team were struggling with changes linked to the merger. I needed guidance on how to help them, since this was only the beginning of things to come. Peter had asked me to work with the Marketing Department to get the next employee satisfaction survey ready. It was much bigger than I had expected, and I was overwhelmed by it.

- *The opportunity that is available to me right now…*

I had talked with Holly about the degree she was pursuing and had discovered that the company reimbursed tuition after the course was completed and an "A" was earned. I didn't have the energy right now to pursue this, but wanted to tuck it away as a goal for the future.

- *I want to use my coach time to…*

  - Learn how to help others manage change
  - Get tips on managing a new project team
  - Determine whether to interview a friend
  - Understand options for my career path

I was closing my journal when Esi approached my office and asked if I had a few minutes. She was one of my more timid employees, but when it came to quality customer service, she soared above the rest, and I had seen tremendous progress over the last few weeks in her sales volume. However, she was often late for work, which was causing problems with her team members. She had recently been given a written warning from my predecessor indicating that she was on probation for her poor attendance.

"Hi, Esi," I responded. "Come in and sit down. What's on your mind?" As she wrung her hands nervously, she said, "I've wanted to come to you for more than a week about my being late for work. Now that I've been given a strong warning about it, I wanted to see if I could change my start time."

This was a difficult question, since we were still short three people. "Esi, I'm not sure we can adjust schedules just yet, since our two new hires aren't out of training, and we're still looking for another person."

She looked very troubled, with watery eyes. "Oh, I see."

I gently asked, "Can you tell me what has been keeping you from being on time?"

"Well, I don't have child care until 7:30 a.m., which means I have to catch the 7:50 bus. It doesn't drop me off here until 8:10, and by the time I get the elevator and log in, it's about 8:20. The earlier bus is at 7:25, but then I'd have to leave my kids alone, and sometimes the babysitter is a few minutes late, and I just can't do that."

I was surprised. Obviously she didn't want to be late on purpose. It seemed that there must be some sort of solution. "Esi, I can understand the dilemma you're in. Is there any alternative other than the bus?"

"I don't drive, nor do I own a car. Taking a taxi is very expensive. My brother can get me to work on his days off, but I'm dependent on the bus the other days of the week."

That certainly explained why she wasn't always late. "Hmmm—does anyone live near you?"

"I don't know. I don't make friends easily. Once I'm here, I try to make up for the time I'm late, so I usually use my breaks to use the restroom, and then get right back on the phones."

I thought to myself that here is a very dedicated single mom with circumstances beyond her control. "Esi, let's see if there is any other solution. Do you mind me asking if you'd be willing to ride with a co-worker if we found someone who lives near you?"

She nodded her head, and said, "I'd be glad to ride with someone. I asked a few people I know on our team, but they live in the opposite direction across town. I just don't know who else to ask."

"Well," I said confidently. "That is something I can help you with. Write down your address for me"—I passed her a piece of paper—"and I'll ask the other supervisors if they know someone who drives in from your area. I'll also ask Scheduling to take a look at shift hours when the new hires are ready to join our team. Maybe there is a way we can start your shift 30 minutes later. And Esi," I paused, "we value the wonderful work you do for our customers, and you're really improving in sales. I'd like to find a way to make this work. Please, this is something you should always feel comfortable talking to me about."

She quickly wrote the address with a few landmarks noted and looked up with a sheepish smile on her face. "Chris, it was easier to talk to you than I thought it would be. I would have come to you sooner, but I thought I could figure it out. I don't like to be dependent on anyone, but I guess I should ask for help when I really need it. Thank you so much," she said gratefully. "I'd better run if I'm going to catch the bus home." She stood up and extended her hand.

I shook her hand and said, "Think about it as partnering rather than being dependent. My guess is that you'll find a way to give back what is given to you."

As Esi walked down the hall, I reflected on my biases. I had jumped to the conclusion that she was not aware of her lateness, and that she had a poor attitude. This certainly was not the case. David interrupted my thoughts. "Earth to Chris," he joked. "What's got you so focused?"

I shared with him the dilemma that Esi was in, and my plan to ask the other supervisors for their help. David replied, "That *is* a big issue. I know several team members on that bus run who are always late. I wonder if we could talk to the bus company to see if they'd be willing to move the time, or put an extra run on that route."

This certainly was a different way to look at it. "Do you think they'd really do that, David?" I asked.

"Well, it couldn't hurt to ask. I know one of the managers at the bus company. I'd be willing to give him a call in the morning and get his reaction to the idea. By the way, where does Esi live?"

"She lives in the new apartments on the west end of the city…," and I continued to describe exactly where she lived.

"Well, I think I have an even better solution. Gerry from my team just moved into those new apartments last week, and he drives to work. They're on the same shift, so I'm sure he'd be willing to give her a ride. I wouldn't mind if some of her awesome service skills rubbed off on him either!" David emphasized. "I can ask Gerry in the morning and see if he's willing to help Esi out."

"Thanks! That was too easy. I owe you one!" I said gratefully. "Let me know what Gerry says, and I'll let Esi know right away."

"Sure thing," David said, "and I will follow up on the bus schedule, too. I have a feeling that we'd have many people less stressed if they could get here on time."

"Thanks again." I added. "See you tomorrow!"

I was glad that we had a potential solution for Esi. I knew that one issue the call center had been struggling with for a long time was adherence to schedule. It seemed that as soon as we had one person turn their habitual tardiness around, it was another person's turn. I added this topic to my chat with Stephanie, and was ready to close the book and get to Lanie's game, on time!

Adherence to Schedule

I was walking into work thinking how proud I was of Lanie. She had improved remarkably and had made her first goal. Even though her team didn't win, it was a big win for her. She was on cloud nine, and I got to see it all and share in her excitement. Now it was time to focus on a very full day, starting out with my meeting with Stephanie.

On the way to Stephanie's office, David stopped to inform me that Gerry was more than happy to give Esi a ride. He suggested that I counsel Esi to offer to pay for half of Gerry's gas; that way he'd be more likely to stay committed to giving her a lift. "That's wonderful. I'll let Esi know as soon as I'm out of my session with Coach Stephanie. Thanks for the quick follow up!"

I sauntered into Stephanie's office with a huge smile on my face.

Stephanie looked up from her computer and greeted me. "Hello, Chris. I'm glad we finally found a time on our calendars to get this coaching session in. Come on in."

I sat down and pulled out my notes, and told Stephanie how David helped me find a ride for Esi.

"That's real teamwork," Stephanie said. "As supervisors, it's critical to have a strong network of different resources for reasons like this one. I'm glad it worked out, and I'm glad we won't lose Esi. She's been working really hard to improve!"

"Yes, I'm impressed by how much she's improved since I set up a development plan with her and have been coaching her during her calls," I said. "I'm wondering, though, how many other associates who are on probation because of adherence to schedule might really be victims of a bigger problem. David told me he thought the bus route was part of the problem and is calling the bus company to see if there is the possibility of an earlier arrival."

Stephanie concurred. "That will help several individuals, but unfortunately, I don't think it will make a difference for those people who are habitually late. You can often see a pattern, since it's the same people who don't come back from breaks on time, or who often call in sick at the last moment. I think child care is part of the issue, but I think it's a motivation or attitude issue for some."

"My dad was in the military so, when I was growing up, he was a stickler for being on time," I said. "I guess I don't understand others who are habitually late. Are there tips on motivation that I could use?"

"That's a good question, but tough to answer," she said. "One person's motivation may not work for another. My suggestion is to think about each of your employees and see if you can determine what motivates them. Once you think you know, ask them to confirm if you're right or wrong. I've done this countless times, and am surprised what I learn."

I thought about this for a moment. I probably knew what motivated about one-third of my team. I said to Stephanie, "I don't think I know what motivates everyone, but I will make it a point to figure it out. Maybe I'll ask others on my team who are late what the cause is, rather than just putting them on probation. If I can help another person like Esi, it's worth it."

"Chris, that's a good idea. May I suggest that you reframe your question just a little bit so they won't feel like you're getting too personal?" Stephanie asked.

"Sure, any way to keep me out of hot water!" I responded.

"Good. How about phrasing it something like, 'I'm looking for ways to motivate everyone to be on time for the start of work and return from breaks. What do you think would work best?'"

What a pro, I thought. "Oh, I see your point," I said. "It's more of a future-focused question, and doesn't judge the other person, but rather invites them to be a part of the solution."

"Yes, exactly," she answered. "You'll hear more information with this type of question and open up very good dialogue. I think you'll also be surprised that not everyone will choose additional pay or more vacation time."

"I'll be very interested in what I learn," I said, then asked Stephanie to repeat her question so I could write it down in my journal.

"Sometimes adherence to schedule may be looked at from a variety of viewpoints," Stephanie continued. "Associates need to clearly understand how non-compliance disrupts the flow of calls. I encourage all supervisors to conduct a 'Learn to Earn' class on the subject so all associates fully understand the importance of being on time and ready to work."

I made another note to put graphs together for my team meeting and to make a suggestion for this topic at our supervisory staff meeting. Watching the clock and wanting to make sure we had time to discuss other topics, I said, "Stephanie, I have three other areas where I need your advice." I quickly shared my accomplishments, and described how I wanted to help my team with managing change. I also wanted tips on being a project leader, Stephanie's opinion about me interviewing a family friend for the open position, and career path options.

Reactions to Change

"Chris, I may need to cut our meeting a little short, so let's get started. If we don't get to everything, I can set up another time with you. These topics could each be a semester-long course," she joked, "but I'll try to give you some insights to get you started. What topic would you like to tackle first?"

I took a split second to think about which topic was most critical. "I'd like to focus on managing change first. I think this will be personally helpful, and I'd love any ideas I can share with my team."

Stephanie replied, "There is a saying that 'change is the only constant we can depend on', so you are wise to begin your journey by learning all you can". She pulled out a thick folder from her desk. "I keep a folder with different articles and worksheets from classes I've taken. Let me share them with you, and point out several that I re-read often.

"You can make a copy of this if you'd like, but let me highlight some of the core information. There are usually four reactions to change." She turned to the board:

- *Denial*

- *Confusion*

- *Loss*

- *Anger*

"Some individuals go into denial and totally withdraw from the organization," she explained. "They lose their initiative as well as their sense of commitment. It's like they've quit, but they stay to perform the tasks without energy or conviction."

"That sounds like one of the team members from my earlier days when the first merger happened," I recalled. "She withdrew a little more each day, and didn't stay up on the latest training, until one day she was so far behind that she really did quit. I remember thinking it was a shame, because she could have done really well."

"When you notice someone is in denial the best thing you can do is to confront them, give as much information as you can, and determine what will help them move through the change," she said. "Sometimes they just need a bridge so they know how to get from the old to the new."

I thought about what Stephanie said. "But what if I don't have all the information or it changes over time?"

"Good point, Chris," she said. "You let them know as much information as you know, and tell them 'That's all I have right now…when I get more I'll tell you.'"

"I see. What about those responding by being very confused?" I asked.

"Confused people need information too," Stephanie explained, "and they want the information put into context for them. They need explanations, guidelines and help exploring the options that the change offers them. They often need help making the transfer to the new until it begins to make sense to them. Otherwise, they scurry around trying to fill in the gaps. It can be a very healthy mode of problem solving, but they can also become so disoriented that they go around in circles, pursuing random activities versus those that will help the organization move."

"I can see myself as you've described," I said. "Sometimes I'll do the most trivial of tasks just to keep my mind off of the change at hand. When Lanie was first born, I did this as I adjusted to being a new parent."

Stephanie chuckled. "Parenting is a perfect example of managing change, because it's constant. Sometimes, depending on the type of change, the circumstances surrounding it, the impact on us at the time, or our past experience with similar change, we may respond differently."

"I agree with you there!" I said. "When I first learned that I had this new supervisor job, I was at a loss for a few days!"

"I remember though, Chris, that you sought out information, and began to make a plan," Stephanie replied. "Many individuals don't know how to seek out information, or how to create a strategy for themselves. That's where you can help."

"I'm not sure I know exactly what to do, but I do know how to listen and clarify information for people. I used to do that all day on the phone!" I said.

"Actually, the ability to understand how people react to change can help customers through changes that are unexpected, or forced on them by virtue of our products or services. The more we can understand the psychology of change, the better we can serve our customers," she said.

"I hadn't thought about it that way, but you're right," I said. "I remember when our lock and key system changed; customers were really at a loss. They took it personally, like the company was trying to make their life miserable and had betrayed them."

"Yes," Stephanie continued, "some people perceive they have lost something that they strongly identified with. They take the change very personally, thinking we no longer value them or their business. They want to go back to the way it was, and don't see the benefits the change offers them."

"Other than explaining what's happening, is there anything else I can do for a person who is feeling lost?" I asked with interest.

"I've had success helping folks find meaningful tasks that are similar to what they're accustomed to, and giving them specific jobs that are useful and needed. At first, I made the mistake of assigning trivial tasks, like cleaning out cabinets or organizing folder drawers. That did more damage, as they perceived that I was quietly taking them out of their real job."

"Thanks for the advice. Hopefully I'll learn from your mistake!" I chuckled.

"I hope so too." Stephanie smiled. "Chris, the last reaction to change is anger. Ironically, while it can be explosive and destructive, anger can also be a healthy way for people to clarify and express their feelings. Anger can be overt, such as yelling, slamming doors, or stomping off mad."

"This sounds like Lanie," I said. "She definitely is a yeller and a stomper. The good news is that I know how she feels. That helps me figure out how to explain my concern, like wearing a skirt that is too short to school."

"You're right," said Stephanie. "However, sometimes anger can be more covert, like sarcasm, sabotage or back stabbing. In any case, anger needs to be addressed and acknowledged so the person is allowed to vent. Sometimes, you'll discover that anger is a "front" for one of the other reactions."

"What happens if I just ignore these reactions, rather than dwell on the change and the negative aspects? Don't people usually get over it eventually and move on?" I asked.

"I don't think ignoring these reactions is the best answer," she said. "Think of it this way: If you went to your doctor reporting a sharp pain in your foot, and the doctor said, 'Let's not dwell on that foot, let's see how the other one feels', you would feel that he is not treating you appropriately. Ignoring change in organizations tells people we don't care, yet being too much of a cheerleader discounts the negative aspects of the experience. The more information, empathy and ideas you can share with others, the more easily they will begin to cope and make the shift to the new."

"I'm clear about the need to address the change, but I'm still at a loss on where to start," I said.

"One of the first steps is to educate your team," Stephanie explained. "You can help them become aware of how they might respond by describing the four reactions to them, and then offer a personal strategy planner. This is my personal copy but you could make up a similar work sheet," she said as she handed me a worksheet that had been written on:

- *GIVENS: The major things I need to ACCEPT as "givens" now.*

- *HELP: The best things I can do to help myself now are…*

- *CHECK: The main things I need to stop doing now are…*

- *SUPPORT: The support that I need is…*

I took a few minutes and jotted these statements down in my journal. Stephanie then handed me another worksheet. "This is a quick way to help people see how they are reacting to a particular change. I've used this during my one-on-one development discussions during a particularly large change, such as this merger. It helps me recognize where each employee is, as well as work with them on their strategy plan."

I looked at the worksheet as Stephanie explained how to use it, and then made a note to introduce the ideas for managing change during my next team meeting.

How You Feel About Change

Instructions: Based on your view of this change situation, rate your feelings using the scale below. For example, if you feel that the change is more of a threat than an opportunity, you would circle either 2 or 4 on the scale.

Threat	2	4	6	8	10	*Opportunity*
Stuck in the Past	2	4	6	8	10	*Future Focused*
Immobilized	2	4	6	8	10	*Activated*
Rigid	2	4	6	8	10	*Flexible*
A Loss	2	4	6	8	10	*A Gain*
Disconnected	2	4	6	8	10	*Connected*
Confusing	2	4	6	8	10	*Clear*
Victim of Change	2	4	6	8	10	*Change Agent*
Reactive	2	4	6	8	10	*Proactive*

"Stephanie, what if I can't handle someone's strong reaction to change? I'm not a counselor, nor do I want to be a psychiatrist," I said.

"Chris, it is a smart move not to get in over your head." Stephanie remarked with seriousness. "We have Employee Assistance Programs (EAP) for that very purpose. If you sense someone is depressed or not coping well, the best thing you can do is to make a referral to a trained professional. Some individuals will not feel comfortable for fear of being labeled, but everything is kept strictly confidential. I actually have walked someone over to the EAP office to give them the courage to ask for help."

"I've never heard of EAP," I said. "Where is the office?"

"It is in Building B. Here is a brochure and telephone extension," she said as she handed me a blue brochure. "Most employees have a presentation about these services during new hire orientation, but it started after you were hired, so you must have missed the announcement."

"I probably received it, but that was before I started getting more organized. Thanks, and I'll be sure to file it where I can find it again!" I put the brochure in the back of my journal and then turned to a blank page, where I wrote "Project Management Tips".

"I know we're racing against the clock, but do we have a few more minutes to discuss project management tips?" I asked.

Just then Stephanie's telephone rang. She glanced over and said, "I'd better get this one. It's Quinn, and she might need something for the meeting." She answered the phone and said, "OK, I'll be there in 30 minutes."

As she hung up the phone, she said, "Chris, you're in luck. Quinn is pushing the meeting back until she has some information from the senior team, so I can be with you for another 20 minutes. What do you want to know about project management?"

Project Management

"I've been asked to lead the customer survey project," I said. "I've got a few ideas on what to do to get everyone organized, but I wanted to hear any tips you have on project management to make this a successful experience."

"Project management is near and dear to my heart," Stephanie said. "Since you like helping people and are good at solving problems, I know you'll be successful. I'm taking a course to become a certified project manager, which is really intense, but I think I can share some key learnings that will help you. Do you have a defined goal for the project?"

"I think I do," I said. "Peter and the Marketing Department want an interim study done to see if our actions are making a difference. Our team thought that if we didn't wait for the annual survey to gauge our progress, we'd have a better chance of influencing positive results."

"That's a good start," Stephanie replied. "Think about stating the goal in terms of what you hope to achieve. Let's say that you're looking for ways to reduce turnover. The goal might be stated as 'Secure approval of policy changes that will cut turnover by 10%'. A specific sub-goal that you might assign to the project team could be 'Develop 5 recommendations to reduce turnover, limiting the implementation cost of each to no more than $1,000'."

"Oh, I see," I replied. "Just be more specific about the expectation of what we need to accomplish, and create very specific sub-goals from there, right?"

"Exactly," she said. "It's easier to manage the scope of a project if the expected goal is very clear. You also won't be caught in the "blame game" around expectations."

I looked puzzled. Stephanie explained, "Let's say the sub-goal was *develop recommendations to reduce turnover.* Stated this way, it's not clear whether to develop a long list of recommendations to eliminate turnover, or just a few.

This process can create a lot of frustration for the person assigned to the task, because the goal is not clear. They interpret, guess, map a course of action, submit it, and may have to do it again and again because it wasn't clarified by the project manager to begin with. This creates an endless cycle of blame, misinterpretation and wasted time. And, it becomes difficult to gain ongoing commitment and satisfaction from the people assigned to a project." She paused as I absorbed her remarks. "So what do you think the expectation is for *your* project?"

I thought about this for a few seconds. "I think it's that we'll have a completed survey by end of next quarter from 20% of our high net worth customers with comparison results communicated by the middle of the following month. How does that sound?" I asked.

"Perfect. Now what are some specific sub-goals you might assign to the project team to reach this overall goal?" Stephanie asked.

"I haven't thought that far ahead yet, but let me see if I can come up with one or two." I thought for a few moments. "I think one of our first sub-goals is to identify the specific statements in the last survey where customers indicated they were less satisfied. Maybe another sub-task would be to determine how we'll select the 20% of customers to be surveyed, and how they will be contacted."

Stephanie beamed at me. "You're getting the hang of it," she said. "So your first job is to do some preliminary work documenting sub-goals you think need to be completed to reach the goal, and then double check with your team to see if there are any others. From there, you'll need to identify which tasks or activities need to happen to accomplish the sub-goal, and assign a time frame and resource to each."

"But what if there are more tasks than people or one item has to be completed before another?" I asked.

"Chris, those are both excellent questions. You may need to determine if all the tasks are critical, or if some can be done simultaneously," she explained. "Sometimes, output from one activity feeds into the start of the next activity. There are several software packages available to help keep track of really complex projects, but I think for your project, you could create a chart with a timeline. You would list your goals, sub-goals and tasks, and the time you think will be required, and then either color code or re-order those that could be completed simultaneously or are dependent on another to be completed first."

I still was confused. "It sounds like some people will be assigned to more than one task," I said. "What if they don't have enough time allocated to accomplish all of the work?"

Stephanie smiled. "Chris, you've uncovered one of the roles a project manager plays in the overall process. You may need to advocate for more time or resources, which may also have consequences on the project budget," she explained. "You need to know who controls the purse strings, and where the project stands on political importance in the company. In other words, who will be held accountable at a senior management level if this project fails or is successful?"

"It sounds like I need to know a whole lot more than I do. I think Peter is my immediate sponsor, but I'm not sure where the purse strings are controlled," I sighed. This was more complicated than I expected. "I don't even know if I have a budget, or how many resources will be available."

Stephanie sensed my anxiety. "It is important that you ask your sponsor, in this case Peter, to share as much detail as he has, especially about budget and resources," she said. "While you're asking him these questions, also be sure that he is in agreement with the goal of the project. Have this conversation early. It will give you clarity and the necessary foundation in case you need to go back and make changes."

I immediately made a note in my journal to schedule a meeting with Peter regarding the customer satisfaction project.

"Chris, I don't think you need to be too concerned about support for this particular project," Stephanie said. "I know it has high importance to everyone at every level. If we don't have quality customer satisfaction, we lose our customer loyalty. And customer loyalty is what keeps us in business! However, I encourage you to do the things we've talked about, and they will also help you manage any project."

"This sounds like wonderful advice. What else should I focus on?" I asked.

"Let me think for a moment." Stephanie paused, and then said, "Chris, another important role that a project manager plays is that of a good communicator. Team members on a project need to be kept up to date frequently and know where they stand as far as achieving the specific sub-goals. Publishing a frequent project schedule update, touching base with people to be sure they aren't experiencing any roadblocks that are preventing them from meeting deadlines, as well as updating your project sponsor on progress are all critical."

I jotted down a quick summary of the points Stephanie made. "It looks like I'll need to brush up my skills on some software to help me keep track of all of these details," I said.

"That's a good idea," Stephanie agreed. "If you find yourself doing more complex projects, you may want to invest in a class on specific project management software to help you manage the details."

I made a note to check around to see what classes were available. "That reminds me. I had a conversation with Holly about how she's working toward her advanced degree in business. I'd like to explore the alternatives for myself." I paused, and then said, "Of course, not right away. I've got enough to learn right now, but Holly described some courses that sound really interesting and may eventually help me on the job."

"Chris, you are wise to be thinking about your future now," Stephanie said. "Make a point to check with Human Resources and ask about the company's tuition reimbursement program. Once you have that detail, we can definitely explore some options that you might consider for your own career path."

"I'll do that" I said, as I jotted another note to myself to stop by the Human Resources office. I looked at my watch and realized I had just 5 minutes remaining of Stephanie's time. "I do have one more question that I'd like to get your opinion on…"

"Chris," Stephanie laughed. "You certainly know how to make the most of every moment. What's on your mind?"

"Well, you know that Tiko and I hired two new associates and that I still have one opening on my team since Charlie was dismissed. A friend of mine left me a message alerting me that he had filled-out an application for the open position, and asked me to recommend him to the hiring supervisor. He doesn't know that the position is for my team. I'm not sure whether it's a wise idea to hire an old friend."

"I can see your dilemma," Stephanie responded, "and there are many pros and cons to this type of situation. First of all, do you think he has the skills to be successful here?"

"I really don't know. We're friends socially since we both played co-ed volleyball for the past few years, but I don't really know his work history."

"The challenge Chris, as you know," Stephanie said, looking at me seriously, "is that he would need to think of you as his boss and you would need to be able to coach him as an employee. My personal experience is that it takes a concerted effort by both parties to make it work. It becomes especially challenging if there is a performance issue, downsizing, or competition for other jobs. Perhaps the first step is to look at his application and determine if he meets the minimum requirements. If he does, then another supervisor could interview him as a preliminary step to see if the job fit is right."

I thought about Stephanie's ideas. "I could definitely take a look at his application," I said. "I could talk with Tiko and explain the circumstances, and see if he'd be willing to interview him, or at least conduct the interview with me to balance any bias I might have." I made a note to speak with Tiko after I obtained the application from Human Resources.

"Chris, I hate to stop us in the middle of this critical decision, but I must leave for my meeting. I have you on my calendar in two weeks for our next meeting," she said.

"Thanks for the extra time Stephanie. As always, you've given me plenty to think about and options to try. I'll see you in a few weeks." I walked back to my office deep in thought.

Implementing Change

When I sat back down at my desk, I re-organized my "to do" from my meeting with Stephanie. I always left my coaching session with her with many answers, but even more questions. I then went to Esi's desk to give her the good news about riding with Gerry.

As I finished giving Esi the details, she said, "Chris, I don't know how to thank you. I think this will work out perfectly. And you will see that I won't be late again!"

I responded, "That's super, Esi. You'll be a perfect role model for the whole office!"

As I left her cubicle, I felt a glow of reward. This part of being a supervisor was all right!

I returned to my desk and started to work on my "to do" list. Once I finished, I went to Tim's cubicle and suggested this might be a good time for me to sit with him and coach him on some calls.

Tim was a bit hesitant, and said, "I'm not having a good day. But if you really want to, I guess it won't hurt."

I wanted this experience to be a good one for Tim. I asked him, "How about if we try it for just 30 minutes, and we'll see how it goes?"

"Sure," Tim said, and began to pull out a head set for me to listen in. "I've been trying some of the questions on the Cheat Sheet, but I'm having a difficult time knowing what question to start with and when to fit questions into the conversation."

"OK, we'll focus on the timing of questions," I said. "What worked for me when I was selling was to listen for something the customer said during the conversation while I was solving their concern that I could use later to introduce a transition question."

Tim still looked confused. "Let me give you an example," I said. "They often talk about their problem with the new key system, and how it's caused them to be late taking their inventory. In that statement, you've heard both the issue about the using the new key system and a timing issue with inventory. Once you've solved the key problem, then you could say something like, 'I'm glad we've got the issue about the key system solved. I know you'll find it goes quicker with practice. Earlier you mentioned that your inventory is late. Are you aware that we have a brand new bar coding program that can be put on all of your products to make inventory go more quickly?'"

Tim's eyes lit up. "I get it," he said. "First, I finish up the call like I normally would with a positive statement about the solution we've reached. Then I use clues I've heard from earlier in the conversation about other needs they may have and turn those into a question. I can do that!"

I was caught up in Tim's enthusiasm. "Super. It's important that the question connects the need you heard to the way in which our product or service will benefit them," I explained. "When I first starting learning how to do this, I used a 'feature dump' rather than a need/benefit question or statement."

Tim nodded in understanding. "Yes, I catch myself doing that when I'm nervous and can't decide what to ask," he said.

"I definitely can relate to that," I said. "I broke myself of that bad habit by making sure I had identified at least three needs before I'd talk about a product. It didn't always work, but was an easy way to eliminate my bad habit. Are you ready to give it a try?"

Tim seemed more relaxed now. "Sure, let's do it!"

Tim pulled out his Cheat Sheet and put it near his computer so it was within eyesight. I listened to several calls, jotting down what I was hearing about potential products or services during Tim's conversation with his customers. He stumbled at first, but began to get the hang of it. After about an hour, and six calls, he had made two sales. He was beaming.

"Those are two sales I would have never made if you hadn't shown me a few tricks," he said. "Thanks!"

"You're welcome. You've been a quick learner. I have time to listen to one more call, and then I'll give you some feedback," I said.

"Maybe the more time you spend with me, the more my sales will go up!" he exclaimed.

I listened to the next customer call, from Mr. Nilhouse, who was very upset that the wheels on his Power Storage mobile units had broken off. He needed the wheels fixed before his next big trade show, which was in two days! Tim handled the call expertly, getting the correct model and size of the unit, and then checking our inventory. He told Mr. Nilhouse that the replacement wheels would be sent overnight at no additional cost so he'd have it time for the trade show. Tim heard the magical hints during the conversation about how rushed and disorganized everything seemed going from one trade show to the other and turned those hints into a sale for two of our higher end products.

As Tim ended the call, I congratulated him and used the CARE model to give him feedback. I said, "Tim, that was awesome! You picked up on Mr. Nilhouse's clue about how disorganized he was and used it to create a needs-based question. When you said, 'I know that keeping all the parts organized so they are easy to find, especially with all of the trade shows you have coming up, and keeping track of the inventory for each show, has been difficult. Our Power Shelf and Inventory Scanner would help you with that. Would you like to hear more about them?' he gave you the go ahead, and ended up buying both products. Keep up those perfect transitions and questions and you may just become our top salesperson!"

Tim had a big smile on his face. "Chris, when will you be back again?" he asked.

"I'm making a commitment to sit in with each person on our team at least once a week. Let me know how it's going—you know practice makes perfect" I chuckled, "and I'll be back to see your progress. Meanwhile, you can be thinking about what else you'd like to work on when I sit with you."

"Sure thing, come by as often as you'd like!" Tim smiled. "I'd better get back to work so I can keep practicing!"

I left Tim's cubicle with a spring in my step. Coaching *willing* associates was definitely going to be one of my favorite parts of the job. I thought, too, that I should keep a list of what each person was being coached on so I could track their progress. I went back to my desk and added a sheet for coaching goals to the folder for each associate on my team, including space for coaching notes.

Mentoring for Career Pathing

As I finished my last folder, I looked up to see Holly standing there. "Hello, how long have you been standing there?" I had been so focused I hadn't heard her approach.

"Just a few seconds," she replied. "You were deep in concentration, so I didn't want to disturb you. Is this a good time to stop by?"

"Perfect time," I said. "I've just finished one of my to-do's!" I went on to explain how well the coaching session went with Tim, and about the tracking system I devised.

"That's good, Chris. Do you mind if I steal your idea?" she asked.

Flattered, I said, "Not at all. Go ahead."

"Thanks," Holly continued. "It will make performance reviews much easier with all of this documentation. You should share the idea at our next supervisor meeting."

"I will. Now, you stopped by for a reason other than to steal my idea. What's on your mind?" I asked.

Holly said that she had an assignment from one of her professors to mentor someone regarding their career path, and to come up with suggested projects, resources and training programs for a development plan. Since earlier I had indicated an interest in her program she wondered if I'd be willing to help her out with this assignment.

"I'd be honored, Holly. I really admire how you've supervised others, including myself, in the past," I said. "In fact, one of my goals is to develop a career path, so this is perfect timing! Any advice you can give me is welcome any time."

"Thanks for the compliment, and for agreeing to help me with my project." she said. "I think we'll both benefit. I'll be sending you some questions to get your feedback on your strengths, as well as opportunities you'd like to focus on. I'll also ask for names of individuals who have worked with you or for you, who would give candid feedback about you. It's called 360-degree feedback, since you try to get information from the circle of people around you. It will be sent to Peter, too, so you get a complete picture."

I was intrigued. "What do the questions ask?"

"The questions are based on various competencies and specific behaviors that make a successful supervisor, manager and director," Holly explained. "For example, one of the questions asks individuals to rate you on how well you demonstrate skills at facilitating groups. Another asks how well you develop timely customer reports for management. The results give us a starting point for our first meeting. We take a look at them together, talk about your goals, and begin the discussion of where you would like to focus your development plan."

"Oh, I see," I said. "I think this will be really helpful, and will make sure I'm headed in the right direction."

Holly looked pleased. "Terrific. Then I'd like to set up a half-hour meeting every week until we finish your development plan," she said, then laughed, "which has to be by the end of the semester, of course!"

We compared calendars, and scheduled half-hour meetings each week for the next two months. Holly thanked me again and told me to be looking for her e-mail.

I sat back, looked at the clock and realized it was near the end of my day. Another action-packed day in the life of a call center supervisor! I stared off as I remembered back to my first day on the job. It seemed like ages ago. At the time I had been so worried about doing this job "by the seat of my pants" that I was uncertain of my own potential for success. And now, two months later, I knew that learning to lead a team would take a combination of learned skill, talent, and a lot of patience—but that I, along with so many others, *would* 'rise to the occasion'. I smiled, looked around my new office and noticed another quote from Stephanie posted to my wall, which said it all.

> *If I have been of service, if I have glimpsed more of the nature and essence of ultimate good, if I am inspired to reach wider horizons of thought and action, if I am at peace with myself, it has been a successful day.*

Alex Noble

APPENDIX #1
Cheat Sheet

Customer Needs	Questions to Ask	Customer Concerns	Product Solutions
Organizer for all parts to support Power Solutions products	How do you keep all of your Power Solutions organized today? Are the appropriate parts quickly found when your customer requests them?	• Busy • Parts not organized	Power Shelf: • One large container/ shelf made to store all sizes • Labeled for easy location • Customized parts
Easy way to keep track of inventory and re-order parts	How do you usually know when you need to re-order parts?	• Inventory is difficult to track • Customers must frequently wait for parts • Lose business because parts are not available	Inventory Scanner: • Bar code automatically scanned at cash register • Daily report for parts sold and those to be re-stocked • Set own parameters for restocking
Customer has limited space to store all necessary products OR Customer needs to bring product to customer site	What space is available for your current products? Room available for new products? Do you own building or rent? How much does the square footage cost you per month?	• Rental cost is increasing • Out of space now or soon • Hassle getting products to large job sites	Power Storage: • Mobile unit on wheels to avoid paying space rent • Automatically organized inside for each piece

165

APPENDIX #2
Customer Associate
Competencies

1 = No indication they have the skill or knowledge
2 = Aware of knowledge or skills, but need guidance
3 = Proficient enough to work independently most of the time
4 = Exhibits high proficiency
5 = Expert

Low	Competency	High	Comments
Unfriendly and/or discourteous, distant, impolite, damages rapport, disrespectful 1 2 3 4 5	**Building Relationships**	Friendly, courteous, easy to talk to, builds rapport and respect, considerate	**FELT** **SAID** **THOUGHT** **DID** **OUTCOME**
Hesitant when faced with new problems, uncertain 1 2 3 4 5	**Confidence**	Self-assured, persistent when faced with obstacles, handles uncomfortable situations well	F S T D O
Difficulty providing appropriate solutions to customer problems 1 2 3 4 5	**Problem Solving**	Provides creative solutions to problems, handles customer requests	F S T D O
Does not resolve issues in a timely manner; does not go extra step to please customers 1 2 3 4 5	**Responsive**	Acts quickly and decisively to solve issues; goes the extra mile to please customers	F S T D O
Pessimistic, easily discouraged; gets defensive when criticized 1 2 3 4 5	**Positive Attitude**	Optimistic, cheerful and looks for positive resolution to problems; open to feedback	F S T D O
Misses key messages; no sense of urgency to situations, insensitive to customer needs 1 2 3 4 5	**Customer Focused**	Listens and acknowledges needs, conveys a sense of urgency, is sensitive to needs	F S T D O
Does not make good business decisions 1 2 3 4 5	**Business Savvy**	Makes decisions that are good for both the customer and the business	F S T D O
Does not work well with others; irritated by others' suggestions and ideas 1 2 3 4 5	**Cooperation**	Works collaboratively with customers and co-workers; is willing to compromise	F S T D O

RECOMMENDED READING

Berry, Leonard. *Discovering the Soul of Service*. New York, NY: The Free Press, 1999.

Canfield, Jack and Jacqueline Miller. *Heart at Work*. New York, NY: McGraw-Hill, 1996.

Caroselli, Marlene. *Leadership Skills for Managers*. New York, NY: McGraw-Hill, 2000.

Hagberg, Janet. *Real Power*. Salem, WI: Sheffield Publishing Company, 1994.

Klinvex, Kevin, Matthew O'Connell, and Christopher Klinvex. *Hiring Great People*. New York, NY: McGraw-Hill, 1999.

McNally, David. *Even Eagles Need a Push—Learning to Soar in a Changing World*. New York, NY: Dell Publishing, 1990.

Simon, Sidney. *Getting Unstuck*. New York, NY: Warner Books Inc, 1988.

Sommer, Robert. *Inspiring Others to Win*. Glendale, CA: Griffin Publishing Group, 1998.

Stone, Florence. *The Manager's Question and Answer Book*. New York, NY: AMACOM Books, 2003.

BIBLIOGRAPHY

Bridges, William. *Managing Transitions: Making the Most of Change.* Cambridge, MA: DeCapo Press, 1991.

Dana, Daniel. *Managing Differences.* Overland Park, KS: MTI Publications, 1996.

Feld, Judy and Ernest Oriente. *SmartMatch Alliances: Achieve Extraordinary Business Growth and Success.* Park City, UT: JumpingJack Publishing, 2002.

Harmin, Merrill. *The Quality Time Way To Go: Practical Strategies to Manage Ideal Days.* Edwardsville, IL: Merrill Harmin, 1986.

Raths, Louis, Merrill Harmin and Sidney Simon. *Values and Teaching: Working With Values in the Classroom.* Columbus, OH: Charles E. Merrill Publishing Company, 1978.

Tuckman, Bruce. *"Developmental Sequence in Small Group",* Psychological Bulletin 63, pp. 384-399.

RESOURCES

Organizations

Incoming Calls Management Institute (ICMI), 130 Holiday Court, P.O. Box 6177, Annapolis, MD 21401. Phone 410-267-0700. Fax 410-267-7010. Contact Brad Cleveland, President.

SQM Group, 4609 23rd Street, Vernon, BC, Canada, V1T 4K7. Phone 800-446-2095. Contact Sarah Kennedy.

ABOUT THE AUTHOR

Anne G. Nickerson

For 25 years, Anne has been developing the potential of people through organizational design, executive coaching and management development activities. She is the principal and founder of Call Center Coach, LLC, and Partners in Development, LLC and is a widely recognized contact center consultant, author, speaker, coach and trainer. Contact her at anne@callcentercoach.com

ORDER FORM

You may obtain additional copies of *Not by the Seat of My Pants: Leadership Lessons for the New Call Center Supervisor* by:

Phone: 888-860-2622   Fax: (860) 871-0334
Mail: Call Center Coach, LLC
    76 Kibbe Road
    Suite 200
    Ellington, CT 06029
E-Mail: holly@callcentercoach.com

Please send me: AMOUNT:

_____ copies of *Not by the Seat of My Pants:*
    Leadership Lessons for the New Call Center Supervisor   _____
    @ $17.95 each

_____ information about Telephone Talk Show Series,   N/C
    Executive Coaching Program and on-site Training

_____ register me for the FREE online newsletter   N/C
    Call Center Insider

_____ provide large volume discount information   N/C

    TAX: Please add 6% for each book being
        shipped within Connecticut.   _____

    SHIPPING: $3 for the first book and $1 for each
        additional book   _____

    TOTAL: _____

PAYMENT METHOD: _____ check   _____ VISA   _____ MasterCard

Credit Card Number: _____   Expiration Date: _____

Name on Card: _____   Signature: _____

Name: _____

Address: _____   Email Address: _____

City/State/Zip: _____

0-595-32366-9